Highly Sensitive Empath

Learn How to Detect the Narcissist Manipulation Techniques and Recover from a Codependent Relationship using Emotional Intelligence and Developing your True Gift

By
Melanie White

© Copyright 2020 all rights reserved.

This document is geared towards providing exact and reliable information with regard to the topic and issue covered. The publication is sold with the idea that the publisher is not required to render accounting, officially permitted, or otherwise qualified services. If advice is necessary, legal or professional, a practiced individual in the profession should be ordered.

From a Declaration of Principles which was accepted and approved equal by a Committee of the American Bar Association and a Committee of Publishers and Associations.

In no way is it legal to reproduce, duplicate, or transmit any part of this document in either electronic means or in printed format. Recording of this publication is strictly prohibited, and any storage of this document is not allowed unless with written permission from the publisher. All rights reserved.

The information provided herein is stated to be truthful and consistent, in that any liability, in terms of inattention or otherwise, by any use or abuse of any policies, processes, or directions contained within is the solitary and utter responsibility of the recipient reader. Under no circumstances will any legal responsibility or blame be held against the publisher for any reparation, damages, or monetary loss due to the information herein, either directly or indirectly.

Respective authors own all copyrights not held by the publisher.

The information herein is offered for informational purposes solely and is universal as so.

The presentation of the information is without a contract or any type of guarantee assurance.

The trademarks that are used are without any consent, and the publication of the trademark is without permission or backing by the trademark owner. All trademarks and brands within this book are for clarifying purposes only and are owned by the owners themselves, not affiliated with this document.

TABLE OF CONTENTS

INTRODUCTION 7
CHAPTER 1: WHAT IS EMPATHY? 9
  What Does This Concept Really Mean? 9
  Do You Have Empathy? 11
  What Prevents Us From Acting With Empathy
  In Our Relationships? 12
  Empathy Goes Through the Path of Self-
  Knowledge 13
  The Science behind Empathy 14
CHAPTER 2: THE DARK SIDE OF EMPATHY 18
  What Is The Advantage When Looking At Each
  Other's Perspective? 19
CHAPTER 3: THE IMPORTANCE OF EMPATHY 23
  How Important Is Empathy In Relationships? 24
  How Important Is Empathy in the Workplace? 28
  Empathy to Overcome Differences 30
CHAPTER 4: TYPES OF EMPATHY 36
CHAPTER 5: HOW TO DEVELOP EMPATHY AND
IMPROVE SOCIAL RELATIONS 40
  The Virtue of Being Empathic 41
  How to Be Empathic 46
CHAPTER 6: WHAT IS CODEPENDENCY? 58
  Signs That You Are In A Codependency
  Relationship 64
CHAPTER 7: UNDERSTANDING NARCISSISTS 69
  What are the causes of this type of disorder? 72
  Narcissistic Personality Disorder Symptoms 74

CHAPTER 8: TYPES OF NARCISSISTS 76
  Other Subtypes of Narcissism 78
CHAPTER 9: NARCISSIST MANIPULATION
TECHNIQUES 82
  Signs of a Narcissist Person 86
CHAPTER 10: NARCISSISM IN RELATIONSHIP 88
  How To Tell If You're Dating A Narcissist? 89
  Tips To Live With A Narcissistic Person 95
  What A Narcissistic Man Has During A
  Relationship 97
CHAPTER 11: HOW TO DEAL WITH
NARCISSISTS 106
  Free your past mistakes 109
CHAPTER 12: NARCISSISTS AT WORK 111
  How to recognize them? 112
  Get to know the narcissist and his weaknesses ... 115
CHAPTER 13: WHAT IS EMOTIONAL
INTELLIGENCE 118
  Emotional Intelligence and Its Components 120
  Features of People with High Emotional
  Intelligence 124
  Emotional Intelligence in Practice and People 125
  Can Emotional Intelligence Be Learned? 127
  How to Measure Emotional Intelligence? 128
CHAPTER 14: HOW TO DEVELOP EMOTIONAL
INTELLIGENCE 129
  Benefits of Emotional Intelligence 135
  Emotional Intelligence at Work: The 5
  Benefits! 138
  Roles Of Emotional Intelligence And
  Teamwork 143

CHAPTER 15: COMMUNICATION WITHOUT WORDS 147
- The Seven Basic Emotions 149
- Micro-Expressions Show the True Feelings 161
- Mimic Point: Error Reading Faces 162
- Facial Expressions: How Do I Know That My Counterpart Is Keeping Something From Me? 164
- Facial Expressions: How They Influence Us 166

CHAPTER 16: EMPATHY A GREAT GIFT AND CURSE. WHAT TO DO WITH EMPATHY? 169
- Unconscious Empathy vs. Conscious Empathy 171

CHAPTER 17: STRATEGIES TO LIVE BETTER 175
- Be highly empathic, when the connection leads to suffering 176
- Visualize how you let each other's emotions go inside 179

INTRODUCTION

The debate about empathy has taken place in academic, investigative, literary, philosophical, pedagogical, clinical, social, political, and market studies, etc. These studies, from various disciplinary fields, do not consolidate a unique sense of the concept of empathy; the differences still persist, which implies that the same term receives a different definition according to the theoretical approach from which it is analyzed.

Eisenberg and Strayer (1987), referring to the difficulties that make the term unique, mention some authors such as Deutsch and Madle (1975), who see empathy as a cognitive process; a Feshbach (1978), Batson and Coca-Cola (1981) and Hoffman (1984), who are primarily affective; Goldstein and Michaels (1985), who regard the psychological therapy as a process with a communicative function.

As an ideal of human relationships, empathy has been conceived in many ways, trying to drive behaviors of cooperation and positive coexistence, together with the need to put oneself in the place of the other, and to be good citizens. Among these we find Leibniz and Rousseau, cited by Wispé (1987).

In the today, authors such as Ruiz and Chaux (2005); Melgarejo and Ramírez (2006); Orjuela, Rozo and Valencia (2010) continue in the same argumentative line. It has also been considered as one of the bases of the moral feelings, according to Adam Smith, quoted by Wispé (1987). Thus, the role of emotions and affection has been emphasized in the moral development of people, he considered empathy as a motivator of altruism, favoring prosocial behaviors, the social cognition, and the aggressiveness inhibitor.

The empathic response includes the ability to understand the other person and put in place, from what is observed, the verbal information accessible from memory (Perspective Taking). In addition, it includes the affective reaction of sharing your emotional state, which can produce joy, sadness, fear, anger or anxiety.

CHAPTER 1
WHAT IS EMPATHY?

Empathy is not only a lovely skill of communication and sharing, but other aspects include how I choose to stand, think, act, communicate and exist. It is a skill that cultivates deep confidence and acceptance within us, which improves the quality of contact with those around us.

What Does This Concept Really Mean?
The term empathy was first introduced by Carl Roger in 1951 and was applied mainly to the educational and psychotherapeutic framework with very positive effects on enhancing one's ability to self-fulfill and for therapeutic change. The question is whether empathy can be applied to everyday life with the same successful results.

In everyday life, empathy is translated as the art of being able to let go of your own world for a while and experience the wants, needs, and feelings of others—seeing through their eyes. That is, to create a true, safe space for the other to be heard, expressed, and exist in the way he wants and decides.

Empathy is a way of deeply listening and interacting with the outside world. It involves the unconditional acceptance of the other's diversity, the uncritical attitude that comes from recognizing the value of the other as a person, and his ability to act, think, and decide in the way that he wants. It may seem easy, but it is not, and this process often requires a deep confrontation with the self.

What Is Empathy?

Empathy is the intention to understand the feelings and emotions, trying to experience objectively and rationally, what another person feels. The word empathy is of Greek origin "empátheia," which means "excited."

Empathy enables people to help each other. It is closely related to altruism—love and concern for others—and the ability to help.

When an individual manages to feel the pain or suffering of others by putting himself in his place, he awakens the desire to help and act according to moral principles.

The ability to put oneself in the place of the other, which develops through empathy, helps one to understand better the behavior of the other person in certain circumstances and the way they make decisions.

The empathetic person is characterized as having affinities and identifying with another person. He knows how to listen to others, and understand their problems and emotions. When someone says "there was an immediate empathy between us," it means that there was a great connection, an immediate identification.

Empathy has been the opposite of antipathy since contact with the other person generates pleasure, joy, and satisfaction. It is a positive attitude that allows us to establish healthy relationships, generating better coexistence between individuals.

Do You Have Empathy?

Think about how often in everyday life, you want to impose your will and to tell others how they should act, think, and feel. Sometimes when others are talking, it may be that you appear to be listening, but in reality you are just thinking about what you will answer. And not by really understanding and listening to them but by correcting them, controlling them, pointing out what they are doing wrong or fixing the problem for yourself.

Sometimes it is because of this that you may violently interrupt because you cannot hear something that is incompatible with you. You become critical of them, raise your voice, feel negative emotions, and are bound to end up in extreme emotional events and actions.

If you remember the important relationships in your family life, at school, and at work, you will find that sometimes it can be difficult to put aside your own position, defend your own opinion, the need to direct, correct, control, and feel that you are superior to others, and instead just listen. How often do we truly let the important people of our lives express their feelings, attitudes, and opinions freely without feeling that they are being directed or controlled? How often have significant others allowed us to do so? How often do we give them and give us the right to decide for ourselves the way we want to live, decide, act, and exist?

What Prevents Us From Acting With Empathy In Our Relationships?
Often the people we interact with tend to have a lot of contradictions with us in the way they think, feel, behave, as well as the way they perceive and sense their reality. People also often tend to see

deficiencies in others and not fully understand or ignore their own.

The deficiencies of others often suppress our own needs for love, acceptance, security, and more. Oppression of our deepest needs, desires, and expectations of others can severely disrupt our relationships with them. This is because suppressing needs often create our negative emotions and thoughts that are difficult to manage, and as a result, we often express them in an explosive and ineffective way.

Thus, an interaction can sometimes be difficult, and unhealthy conflict and communication often occur. If you look more closely, you will realize that this constant attitude is gradually hampering relationships and genuine human communication, and as a result, it will drive away rather than unite. In such a context, how do we to fit an emotional attitude in life?

Empathy Goes Through the Path of Self-Knowledge

True empathy in everyday life is a difficult road, continuous and with ups and downs, a destination rather than a given situation. It is a path that is gradually achieved through constant reflection and understanding of the self. The empathy towards others first stems from the cultivation of the ability to hear, listen, and accept ourselves, not as perfect but as beings with weaknesses and strengths.

Empathy in our daily contacts means not only the ability to listen, but the ability to hear when we need to talk, when to remain silent, and the way we communicate in order to become richer through the diversity of others. To experience the relationship and our contact with others, to learn, not to teach, to open up through communication and not to be locked into our rigid world. Only then can we be better able to accept and empathize with others as a whole in our lives, let go of the ego in us and make our relationships more profound and meaningful.

The Science behind Empathy
1. The neuronal mirror system

The researchers discovered a special group of brain cells responsible for the feeling of compassion. These cells enable us to reflect emotions, to feel each other's pain, fear, or joy. Because we are considered to have hypersensitive neuronal mirrors, we experience the emotions of those around us very strongly. How does this happen? Neuron mirrors are triggered by external stimuli. For example, if our partner is hurt, we feel hurt ourselves. Our child is crying; we feel sadness too. Our friend is happy; we are happy too. On the contrary, psychopaths and narcissists are thought to have what science calls a "defective emotion disorder." This means that they lack the ability to feel as well as all other people, a feature that may be due to the neuronal mirror dysfunction. We have to be careful with these people because they are unable to give unconditional love.

2. Electromagnetic fields

The second finding is that both the brain and the heart create electromagnetic fields. According to the HeartMath Institute, these fields convey information about people's feelings and thoughts. We are very sensitive to this information and tend to be overwhelmed by its volume and intensity. We also tend to feel more strongly in our bodies the changes in the electromagnetic field of the earth and the sun. Emotions know well that what happens on earth and in the sun affects our mood and energy.

3. Emotional infection

The third finding that helps us understand empathy is the phenomenon of emotional contagion. Research has shown that many people grab the feelings of those around them. One baby's crying, for example, can trigger a wave of crying in a hospital ward. A person who expresses high stress in the workplace can also spread it to their colleagues. People easily catch the feeling of others belonging to the same group.

4. Increased sensitivity to dopamine

The fourth finding relates to dopamine, a neurotransmitter that enhances neuronal function and is associated with response to pleasure. Research has shown that inbound sentiments tend to be more susceptible to dopamine than inbound ones. Essentially, they need less dopamine to feel happy. This could explain why they feel more comfortable spending time with themselves, reading and meditating while needing less external stimuli such as partying and other crowded gatherings. On the contrary, extroverts are thirsty for dopamine and, therefore, excited about the events. In fact, it never satisfies them.

5. Sensitivity

The fifth finding, which I find particularly fascinating, is an extraordinary condition called "emotional reflection." This is a neurological condition in which two different senses are combined in the brain. For example, you see colors while listening to a song or feel the taste of words. Famous sentiments include Isaac Newton, Billy Joel, and violinist, Itzhak Perlman. However, with emotional reflection, people can feel the feelings and physical sensations of others as if they were their own. This is a wonderful neurological explanation of the experience of an emotional one.

Research says: Empathy is the most valuable human quality. With these dizzying rhythms we live in, it's easy to get exhausted. Even so, empathy is the quality that will help us. It will enable us to respect each other even when we disagree. Empathy does not make us emotionally crippled, nor does it deprive us of our critical ability. Instead, it allows us to keep our hearts open, and to show tolerance and understanding. It may not always be effective in interpersonal relationships and bringing peace to the world, but I think it's the best solution we have.

CHAPTER 2
THE DARK SIDE OF EMPATHY

According to a new study, we need to be careful when trying to understand how people feel and think. It is often said that the key to empathy is to try to get into the other person's "shoes." On this basis, once we understand the other person's perspective, we can anticipate his feelings and behavior, thereby reducing the gap between ourselves and the other. This "theory of mind" begins to develop from our childhood and accompanies us throughout our lives, helping us to develop our social relationships.

But sometimes it is ineffective to understand each other, and because people cannot read the minds of others, words help us. Specifically, when we ask what we want and the answers we receive for what we ask.

Psychologists have conducted several studies to check whether getting into someone else's "shoes" makes people more accurate in predicting the feelings and thoughts of others. In the surveys, participants were asked to "guess" how someone felt in their eyes or to find out if their smiles were false or not. Some of the participants were given various instructions on how to do it, to concentrate, to empathize with each other, to imitate his or her facial expression so that they could more easily get into position before making predictions about how he or she felt. Others were not instructed.

In the findings of the investigations, there was no difference in the performance of those who received and did not receive the instructions. On the contrary, sometimes, those who accepted the instructions did worse, proving that sometimes seeing one another's perspective does not work the way we think. Many times we judge each other's experiences based on our own information and use stereotypes that are not accurate. However, when we go into the process of thinking, another perspective helps us to be less self-centered, does not confuse our own emotions with the feelings of others, and helps us to question the accuracy of our assumptions about each other.

What Is The Advantage When Looking At Each Other's Perspective?

In other couples' surveys, participants were asked to enter their partner's place and guess their preferences or opinion about movies, art, jokes, videos, social issues, or even to dress up. They were also asked to answer how confident they feel about their cases and how well they know the person they are dealing with.

Psychologists wanted to study whether in real life, getting into the position of someone we are close to is more expensive. The results showed that again, participants who received some instructions did not do better than those who did not receive them; on the contrary, they did worse sometimes. The time frame they knew the other person seemed to have no correlation. Although you would assume that when you know the other person and get into their position, such as a friend or partner, the results will be more accurate and effective. However, it seems that acquaintance is not helpful.

Of course, these findings do not mean that it is of no value to try to experience the other person's perspective but that it is not worth the effort we give it. Instead of constantly appreciating each other's experiences, we can come closer to them. The findings also show that adopting the other person's perspective enhances social relationships. But this is not always good.

For example, as the lead researcher points out, seeing the perspective of a serial killer or a member of ISIS can make us feel closer to them, but that is not a positive outcome. He also states that psychologists' researchers often interpret their findings through their own value system, political beliefs, and ethics.

Want to know how someone feels? Just ask him

If putting ourselves in the other's place does not always work correctly, then what is the element that enhances precision in interpersonal understanding? In a recent experiment, psychologists studied another strategy. Before responding, participants were asked to either imagine how the other would feel or to ask him about films, art, or anything else they were asked to answer. Those who gathered more information guessed more accurately each other's preferences.

However, they were not more confident in their predictions about others, thus showing that people value the importance of being in the other's place and underestimate direct communication. People have misunderstood what the most effective strategies to understand others are. Although trusting one's instincts and intuition matters a lot to people, as a lead research psychologist says, it often leads to mistakes in the intentions of others.

He also stresses that humans are the most social kind on the planet. The problem is that we think we understand others better than we actually understand them, so we come to conclusions that are not accurate.

He cites an example in which he tried to console one of his best friends whose father died. Because he had lost his parents years ago, he thought he understood her pain. But when he showed his compassion, he blocked himself. Her father's death was unexpected, and she felt no pain but peace. So instead of making the assumption about how she feels, he could have just asked her how she feels.

Whether we are talking about our own spouse or a politician, we are more likely to really understand him if we simply ask him to explain his point of view and listen to him.

To become good at interpersonal understanding does not require doing good things but becoming a good "journalist." To learn, that is, to put people in a position where they will answer questions honestly and openly.

CHAPTER 3
THE IMPORTANCE OF EMPATHY

Carl Rogers, the inventor of the person-centered method, established the term "empathy." He defined it as the therapist's ability to hear and feel the other's feelings, to perceive the connections and meanings that exist in the other's words and behavior. Empathy encompasses acceptance of the other, total respect of his experience and personality, without interpretation, criticism, and evaluations. It is the warmth and security that the therapist provides the patient with knowing, expressing, and investigating the voices that are within him. The healer is often reluctant to let go and experience this freedom, many times having never experienced it again. But then, having built a relationship of trust, he begins to try and get tested.

Throughout this process, the therapist is next to the patient and accompanies him, showing respect, acceptance, and an attitude of empathy. It is important to say that empathy happens in a climate of non-direction, as the goal is to synchronize the therapist with the patient's experience. It is not intended to guide, plan, or accelerate the process. Not used as a technique, it is an attitude for the therapist to help the patient feel safe, accepted, and to better clarify their experiences.

With a compassionate attitude, we can better respond to the wishes of the patient, as we can know him/her "close" and "within," so in an indirect way we accompany the patient, and after listening to his/her wishes, we intervene to facilitate him/her. Michel Lobrot, the founder of Non-invasive directional (NDI), contrasts with Rogers, saying that there is no need to intervene.

We have a responsibility to intervene but in the direction of the healer!

So being focused on the other person, empathetic, and listening to his wishes, we can intervene by supporting the patient wherever he wants to go. Through this process, the healer feels the security and support to develop his potential, to try new ways of living, allowing himself and others greater freedom, acceptance, and love.

How Important Is Empathy In Relationships?

In social language, empathy means the emotional capacity to feel what someone else would feel if I were in the same situation as their own. It is the ability to understand feelings and emotions, trying to experience what the person with whom I relate feels. It is not enough just to project ourselves into the situation one is living in and understanding their pain or suffering intellectually. This is sympathy. Sympathy is an intellectual behavior, and empathy is an emotive fusion behavior. Being a sympathetic person is choosing to be in the presence of others, to be considerate, to please them because we have affinities with the situation they are living with and with themselves.

What is empathy for? How important is empathy in our relationships?

First, it is important to say that we are not born empathic but become empathic people. This means that empathy is not a personal trait but a behavior that can be learned. It is the behavior to put ourselves in the other's shoes, identify with another person or their situation, know how to listen to each other and strive to understand others' problems, difficulties, and emotions, and to be useful to others. Empathy is a social, behavioral skill needed to have a positive, pleasurable, fulfilling, and quality relationship.

That said, we come back to the questions. Our attitudes affect people positively or negatively, and we will be affected by their reactions to the behaviors we emit in relation to them. It is a social context of action and consequence between two people in any kind of relationship (family, friendship, dating, and marriage). So empathy serves to acquire and maintain a quality relationship with someone.

The first importance of empathy in relationships is to form bonds with people. Without the bond, no relationship is built or evolves positively. We have no desire to relate to people who do not act attentive, caring, and welcoming to each other. Therefore, we avoid contact with these people and do not bond with them. The second importance of empathy is that through empathy, we can better understand the behavior of others and how someone else makes decisions. This understanding of the other helps us to know how it works, and how we should relate to this person if we are to have a good relationship with them. What they like, dislike, what they tolerate or don't tolerate, what irritates them, or makes them happy... When we meet the person we relate to, we increase the chance of success in the relationship, of feeling happiness, comfort, and well-being. The third importance of empathy is that we have the emotional capacity to help people according to their moral principles. Empathy sensitizes and motivates people to want to approach and help each other.

To be empathic, we must be able to overcome the barriers of selfishness, prejudice, or fear of what is unknown or different. For one person to be able to act empathetically, one has to take attention away from one's own problems and keep one's focus on the other person. This is a big challenge in affective relationships, especially since we live in a society that teaches and motivates people to think first about themselves and meet their needs over the other, when we should really think about each other first, to make others happy—and feel good. When we do this, the consequences of our behavior motivate the other person to treat us well, make us happy, value us, and love us. As long as the philosophy of life is thinking of yourself, relationships will continue to be abused and broken, and people will be unhappy in their relationships. Empathy cannot be exercised with the intention of receiving something from the person I am empathetic with. Using empathy as a behavioral strategy to receive attention, affection, and help will only trigger frustration, suffering, and distress in the relationship. Empathy works when it is genuine. No one owes you anything for being empathetic with someone. The consequence of being empathic is that we feel good, happy, and satisfied that we have the ability to be helpful to those who need us. When we have this conduct in relationships, we receive much more from the other than we imagine and in a very natural and spontaneous way. This dynamic strengthens relationships.

Therefore, empathy is an indispensable behavior to improve the quality of communication and relationship between people. We can exercise empathy by training ourselves to have and keep a watchful and affectionate eye on the needs of the people with whom we relate, to help them. If we want to feel happy and have a successful relationship, we need to be empathic.

How Important Is Empathy in the Workplace?

Work is a great place for empathy. In private and professional life, a guarantee of positive communication is the expression of emotions and needs and a willingness to understand others. Only then can you establish a real relationship that will bring professional success:

Empathic work

We work because we want to meet our needs. Mainly, to earn money and ensure a dignified life. The work also allows you to meet other needs: self-development, self-improvement, acceptance, achievement of professional goals and ambitions, being part of the team, and a person appreciated and noticed. When the performance of duties is a source of satisfaction and fulfillment in life, it is no longer just a job, but the fulfillment of our key needs. This gives us a better feeling of well-being. As a result, we are more responsible, independent, and willing to take challenges.

Awareness of our own needs supports the fight against the main enemies of communication: expressing needs with violence. When we learn about our expectations and requirements as well as pros and cons, we accept ourselves more and learn to receive criticism without strong emotions. Criticism often becomes a reason for quarrels and misunderstandings at work. Nobody likes to be criticized, but when we accept the imperfections, we realize that the person who criticizes us is not the enemy. Therefore, empathy, i.e., talking about emotions and needs, and their acceptance, are necessary skills in the workplace. When we look at the issue from a different perspective, we can discover a phenomenal solution to the problem and show off the idea.

It is also important to take full responsibility for your emotions. Each of them is the result of satisfying or not satisfying one of the needs.

Road to empathy at work

To use empathy in the workplace, you have to: speak without judgment—when you are out of control over your emotions and evaluate what you see and hear, you can have a destructive effect on communication. Describe the situation impersonally without any emotional terms. Also, try to empathize with the other person's situation. Therefore, do not judge quickly and on impulse. Emotions tend to be the worst advisor; talk about your feelings and needs—do not hide how you feel, just say directly how the behavior of the other person directly affects you; talk about what to do to make it better—in work and everyday life you need to look for the best solutions, and simplify and improve ideas; listen and hear what others are saying—thanks to this you will receive feedback and understand it. An active listener is a good employee because he strives to understand not only himself but also his colleagues.

Empathy to Overcome Differences
We live according to our own experience of reality, with a unique vision of the world. It seems a truth. However, we have a hard time understanding this basic principle of subjectivity: we see the world through our eyes. Our perception is limited by our

senses, history, belief systems, temperament and moods. The reality that we assume objective and unilaterally apprehensive is not only biased but constructed from our identity and circumstances.

Therefore, it is essential for our individual development and as a society that we learn to see the world according to the eyes of others. This is only possible through empathy, understood as the ability to interpret and experience the world from the point of view of the other person. Empathy, then, is an intentional and active attempt to try to understand the worldview that the other person has, their emotions, thoughts, and, ultimately, their reality. A reality that, like ours, is also biased by its identity and history.

Human beings are primarily sociable, and in our language and ability to communicate, that essence is manifested. But communicating is not just talking; it also implies the possibility of understanding the emotional states of the other. And communication is vital to maintain healthy relationships. For this, it is crucial to give the entity into the perception of the other and understand that their vision of reality is as valid as ours, even if we do not share it.

From the neuro-psycho-biological point of view, our ability to empathize is inherent in brain activity. The area that assists in the process of empathy is the right supramarginal gyrus, designed to help us distinguish our emotional state from others, with a fundamental role in our ability to decipher what the other may be feeling. It seems that there is a neuronal synapse system that acts as a mirror, somehow reproducing the behaviors of others.

This could explain why when someone yawns, we yawn too. But this process becomes even more complex when it has to do with emotions, as long as it seems to produce a kind of mimesis or reflex. If we see someone feeling pain or joy, we project that emotion in ourselves, experiencing, in some way, the same feeling. Emotions are contagious, so it is crucial to know your own and understand others.

Brain reactions are marked by unintentional, unconscious processes. To promote empathy and improve relationships, it is necessary to make them conscious and deliberate. In other words, to be truly empathetic, one must go beyond the neurological reflex and make a conscious effort to think beyond oneself.

Like almost anything else, empathy is a habit that can be perfected through practice. The rules of empathy are quite simple and include, for example, observing others. We tend to spend most of our time worried and busy with our own issues, on the phone or the computer or prisoners of our routine. Taking the time to observe others can be a great challenge, but it is crucial to the development of empathy. Observe, look, discover, decode, and try to understand what the other person thinks and feels. See beyond your nose and try to decipher who that other is, what battles he is fighting, how he is, or what happens to him. Moreover, overcome the challenge and ensure that these answers matter to us, really and genuinely. See and appreciate, instead of prejudging, categorizing, or denying. Having a healthy curiosity about the other, to build it, not destroy it, that is empathy.

Another essential step to becoming more empathetic is to listen.

HEAR! Most of the time, conversations—especially those high pitched or quarrelsome—tend to be more verbal combat than a genuine exchange of ideas, with the interlocutors formulating answers before letting the other finish speaking. Speaking without listening, speaking to respond, or counter-argument is very different from listening with empathy. To truly understand what happens to the other, one must learn to stop, listen and take the time to respond, process what the other says and learn to exchange opinions in a healthy and constructive way. Before trying to impose our point of view, let's ask questions to clarify the perspective of the other, trying to understand what he meant, what his motivations are, what he feels, what he believes, what assumptions he has, what experiences led him to be who he is.

Communicating does not imply agreeing, and it is not necessary to share a point of view to understand and recognize it. When we really listen, we can improve and amplify our own interpretation and complete our biased and partial worldview. The disagreement may be a complement to our perceptual incompleteness. It is said that empathy is to put yourself in each other's shoes and think about what you would do instead. However, it is more accurate to understand that empathy is to understand what puts the other in his place.

Another rule of empathy is to be flexible and set aside rigid beliefs.

Accept that the opinions of others are as valid as yours. Learning from the other person and recognizing other ways of being, thinking and feeling, enriches, and improves our perspectives. It is also important to open and express our thoughts and emotions. For that, it is essential to know yourself, that old Socratic proverb. It may sound unlikely, but, many times, we don't know what we truly think or feel, let alone how we can communicate it.

Empathy implies challenging prejudices and stereotypes without judging the one who is different as an enemy.

It is essential to get out of the "we versus those who think differently" dynamic. These labels not only prevent us from growing as individuals, but they stagnate us as a society.

Empathy is a reciprocal issue, based on mutual understanding, observing and being seen, paying attention, and being heard. No one owns the truth. No one. Moreover, we build the truth among all, despite the discrepancies. After all, there must be something in common that allows us to overcome differences and enrich ourselves with them.

CHAPTER 4
TYPES OF EMPATHY

People with empathy are rare human beings who give the impression that they carry the weight of this world. Their souls are among us for one simple reason, to strike the perfect balance in this universe.

They are the people who care and listen to us. People whose halo shines bright and attracts everyone else. Those who are well aware of the environment around them and cannot stand the wilderness.

A soul with deep empathy in this world offers many benefits and benefits but can sometimes overwhelm a person, leaving him or her empty and disoriented.

That is why it is so important to find a way to define and give a name to what we are experiencing in order to better understand our nature and to recognize those who have the same abilities as us.

These are the types of empathy that are recognized everywhere around us.

1) The pure perceptual empathy

These kinds of separate souls have the ability to simply know something or find the right answer to a question that usually confuses others.

The "lamps" of their imagination are easily and constantly lit with sudden vivid ideas... It is the intuitive ability of clear knowledge.

2) Naturally receptive empathy

These individuals are known to be very sensitive and perceive the physical suffering of others. They feel our illness and physical pain. They are easily depleted when they are with sick people. The stress, pain, and feelings of others can affect them and easily manifest in their bodies.

3) Sensitivity to fauna

Someone in this category is recognized for his ability to understand an animal's mental state and emotions to the extent that it can interact and positively influence its behavior.

These individuals have a distinct connection to the animal world, and because of this, they can receive the energy sent by them. They are known to love animals more than humans and to have a deeper mutual understanding of all kinds of animals.

4) Germanic Empathy

It is also called environmental compassion. It represents a person's ability to feel and be miraculously attracted to certain places. People with Germanic Empathy can feel the sadness or happiness that exists in one place.

They are often drawn to old houses, graves, or churches for no reason. They feel the spirit of a particular location and the events that have happened. They are very attached to the natural world and mourn the destruction that others are causing.

5) Spiritual Empathy

People with Spiritual Empathy have established a deep connection with the deceased and the supernatural. They have the ability to feel or hear the thoughts or mental impressions of the spiritual world.

They are known to be hypersensitive to the high-frequency actions that some people have.

6) Predictive Empathy

These people have a strong sense of intuition. They have visions of events that are going to happen.

Forecasting is the ability to predict a situation that will happen—the power of being able to see something that is not even there and anticipate it.

These visions of the future are most often presented in their dreams. They dream of reality. We can still say that they are the creators of their realities.

Their dreams are of two kinds: those in which they can see exactly what is going to happen and those with signs of a future event.

7) Telepathic Empathy

These individuals have the power to read and decipher one's expressive thoughts.

8) Psychometric Empathy

This kind of empathy is manifested in a person's ability to receive energy, memories, and important information from natural objects such as jewelry, clothing, and photographs.

Having and taking care of these abilities can make a person feel worn out and exhausted. However, it is very important to recognize that the unusual abilities that these people cultivate make the world thrive.

CHAPTER 5
HOW TO DEVELOP EMPATHY AND IMPROVE SOCIAL RELATIONS

"You never have the patience just to sit and listen." "All you always want to do is try to fix things." "You just don't understand how much it hurt when you said that." Judgments like these and many others verbalized or thought in the context of interpersonal relationships often point to a popular problem: lack of empathy for the other.

Empathy is a condition of functional interpersonal relationships. In personal contexts, including marriages, relationships, friendships and parental relationships, as well as in professional contexts such as management, professional clientele, student-teacher and peer relationships, being empathic with the situations of others can promote trust. This leads to open and honest communication, thus facilitating the resolution of interpersonal conflicts and constructive change.

In fact, the recent work on emotional intelligence by Daniel Goleman suggests that emotional intelligence, one's emotional quotient (EQ), which includes empathy as a core component, can sometimes be more important than the intelligence quotient (IQ).

The initial investigation carried out by Carl Rogers was on the importance of empathy in building trust in psychological and psychotherapeutic relationships, as well as in creating self-report inventories designed to measure the empathy ratio (EQ).

The Virtue of Being Empathic

First, it is essential to distinguish between empathy as a mental state and empathy as a trait or disposition of the character. The first relates to the second as those who are empathic as one of their character traits will tend to experience states of empathy in relation to the difficulties of others.

As a mental state, empathy implies resonating with what is happening in the subjective world of another. Let's call the person with whom you identify, the goal/objective of your empathy. Now, when you identify with someone, you not only know what the objective is going through, but you also feel it, although, as Rogers would say, "without losing quality, 'as if'," that is, without losing your objectivity as an observer.

Then, a friend of yours has just lost her father; and, although you may not have lost a father, you can still empathize. So, to know what it would be like to lose a father, you can imagine the harsh reality of not being able to see, trust or experience the love and support of someone who has played such an important role in your life. You can imagine what it would be like to lose your own father, even if you've never had the real experience.

This is what it means to "put yourself in the shoes of the other person." And doing so can lead you to emotionally appreciate the loss as if it had happened to you, again, without losing this quality "as if." The emotional response here will include the somatic sensations that can normally accompany the loss of a loved one, such as a hollow feeling in his stomach, a lump in his throat, and watery eyes.

Then you will also have certain behavioral tendencies associated with such sadness.

However, some people do not seem to resonate very well with the experiences of others. While they may understand their circumstances, they may not have the required emotional response. Even other people may lack the understanding of what a person may be going through, as well. In fact, it can be said that some of us are more empathetic than others, which means that some are likely to empathize more often than others.

Keep in mind that by saying that some people are more empathetic, I don't want to say that some people have higher quality empathy experiences than others. As a personality trait, empathy is more like being pregnant, which is like being overweight.

People are not more or less pregnant. They are either pregnant or not. In contrast, people may be more or less overweight. Being empathetic does not admit degrees. You are either being empathic or not.

To the extent that it lacks any of the cognitive, emotional, or behavioral components necessary for empathy, it lacks empathy. Therefore, the person who feels emotionally disturbed by the bad news of another person does not feel empathy if he or she does not really understand or appreciate what the bad news really is; and, conversely, the person who knows and appreciates what has happened, but simply does not feel it, also lacks empathy.

So the question of how to be more empathetic becomes the question of how to more frequently achieve the cognitive, behavioral, and emotional synergy that is involved in empathy.

Also note that empathy is not simply a list of independent cognitive, behavioral, and emotional variables; it is a balance of such factors that one is thinking, feeling, and inclining to conduct in ways that support each other.

Therefore, there is an interaction between these factors. The thought of your friend in such emotional pain provokes your own painful sensations, and these feelings, in turn, inform and transform your thoughts, particularly your qualification or evaluation of what happened ("How can such a good person suffer like this!")

In addition, people who can be said to be empathic are people who tend to be empathic. That is, empathizing sometimes does not make someone an empathetic person, but telling the truth sometimes makes someone truthful.

Because, an empathetic person, like the truthful person, has a habit of being empathic. That is, when others are suffering, they tend to experience empathy for their difficulties. This does not mean that empathic people should always feel empathy in such cases, and truthful people should always tell the truth.

However, when the lack of empathic consideration becomes more the rule than the exception, then it is clear that the person in question is not usually willing to empathize.

In addition, the analogy with being truthful is also revealed in another way. Empathy, like truthfulness, can be properly considered a moral virtue. According to Aristotle, moral virtues involve the balance of cognitive, behavioral, and emotional factors. The morally virtuous person is someone who exerts a rational restriction on the indulgences of appetites and actions.

Similarly, an empathic person applies their knowledge of the difficulties of others to report their emotional responses to these situations and acts in line with those enlightened emotions. For example, knowing how someone became homeless: the loss of a job, being evicted from their apartment as a result of not being able to pay the rent, not having an address that affected their ability to find another job, etc. can inform the sadness that one experiences from the plight of the homeless and can help motivate one to do something about it.

Now, Aristotle maintained that one attains virtue through practice. Thus, people learn to be sincere, brave, and simply telling the truth, doing brave things, and treating others fairly. Similarly, being empathetic requires practice. To become empathetic (that is, cultivate the virtue of empathy), you must work on it by being empathetic.

How to Be Empathic
1. Focus your attention on the well-being, interests, and needs of others.

As stated, there is a cognitive component to empathize with another. That is, there is some knowledge that you must have to empathize with the other person. First, one does not simply sympathize with another person; rather an empathy with another about something.

That which is what empathy is all about can be properly called the subject of empathy. Now, the issue of empathy is always an event or state of affairs that is contrary to the welfare, interests, or needs of the objective.

By "welfare," I mean the promotion of happiness (pleasure and absence of pain and suffering). By "interests," I mean desires and goals held seriously, life plans, and rights. By "needs," I mean things like food, clothing, and shelter. (Non-physical "needs," such as love, intimacy, freedom, autonomy, friendship, and belonging, include them in interests.)

Any event that affects the welfare, interests and needs of others also counts as relevant knowledge to empathize.

Therefore, if you know that another has lost a loved one, this fact counts as relevant knowledge; but also, if you know that the beloved was killed by a drunk driver, that fact is also relevant. Why? It is because this fact explains the loss.

Actually, the fact that this individual has been hit by such an unexpected, unnecessary, and unforeseen act helps clarify how traumatic the event should be for the purpose. Therefore, the subject of empathy always consists of facts (or claims of facts) about any event or state of things adverse to the welfare, interests, or needs of the objective, including the facts (or claims of facts) relevant to this adversity.

2. Key in shared human values.

Such an ability to enter the welfare, interests, and needs of others also requires the ability to take the perspective of another person's value. For example, most of us can appreciate the difficulty of losing a dear relative.

But what if the beloved family member is a pet, say a goldfish? Here, even if you don't regret the death of a goldfish yourself, you may still know how it feels to lose someone you love, so your empathy powers can extend to the loss of the target.

In a general sense, the issue of empathy, in this case, is about the loss of a loved one, which is a shared human value. Similarly, one does not need to be gay to empathize with a gay person about their partner's sexual infidelity. Empathy, therefore, implies the ability to enter shared human values in various interpersonal contexts and cultures.

This value dimension of empathy is an integral part of the emotional component of empathy. By simply understanding the facts related to the subject of empathy, one is not involved in the subjective world of the objective. One cannot feel what is happening.

To be empathetic, you must also "feel bad" about the plight of the target. Here they are not simply entertaining facts; you are also rating or evaluating them. You are evaluating the evil of what is happening in the objective: the suffering, the anguish of not being accepted by your partners; the loss of a loved one; the painful understanding that the love of your life has been unfaithful; the fear of losing one's livelihood; the frustration of repeatedly having bad luck; and so on.

To get to this place, you must identify with misfortune in terms of the shared human values that are at stake. This is where you put yourself in the place of the objective and imagine how you would feel if you were facing an identical situation.

From this phenomenological position, you are not yet the other person, but you are still (psychologically) there, facing the same adversity. From this perspective, you can appreciate what the objective is going through because now you share the misfortune. Their evil is now evident from this shared, interpersonal, and phenomenological perspective.

3. Suspend your own judgments and criticisms considered.

The pronouncements and clichés about overcoming it and moving forward will not bring you closer to the subjective world of the objective. You will not feel pain or anguish, or the tension in your own muscles. To do this, you must do without your own analysis and criticism, and you should not focus on how to fix things.

In this sense, empathy is antipragmatic. If you approach the goal with an eye on fixing what is wrong, then you will not share the experience of what is (or seems to be) wrong. You will miss the opportunity to empathize. Also, people who are suffering may not even want their confidants to help fix anything, at least not yet.

They may simply want someone to know what they are going through. The solution to the problem may arise after empathy has helped establish a good relationship and trust.

This does not mean that you must accept the perspective of the objective or his value assessments; however, in the process of empathy, you must dispense with your own qualifications, analysis, evaluations, and criticisms to obtain subjective access to the subjective world of the objective.

Of course, this can be very difficult if the subjective world of the objective is perverse or bad. This is the reason why most of us lack empathy for child molesters and mass murderers.

4. *Connect with the target.*

Suspending your own value judgments, while placing yourself in the subjective shoes of the objective, is essential to empathize. This mental approach is what feminist psychologist, Blythe Clincher, calls "connected knowledge."

The heart of connected knowledge is the imaginative attachment: try to get behind the other person's eyes and "look at it from that person's point of view." You must suspend your disbelief, set aside your opinions, try to see the logic in the idea. Ultimately, it is not necessary to agree with it. But while you're entertaining it, you should ... "say yes." You must empathize with her, feel, and think with the person who created her.

To obtain such knowledge, therefore, you must ruin yourself to see the truth in what the objective says. "I can see how difficult it has been for you to overcome your ex; how much you still love her, I can understand how much you want to be together again and how the idea of her being with someone else is so painful."

Here you are resonating with the target values. These values (unrequited love, jealousy, sadness, and lack of power) are shared human values. As such, it can "connect," on a human level, "with the objective of sharing these values."

This contrasts with what Clincher calls "separate knowledge," which approaches the target with doubt and disbelief to deny what it is saying. "I don't see how you can continue to love her after what she has done to you." "What he needs now is to get a good lawyer, so he doesn't take it to clean."

By adopting this last approach, you will not feel empathy; you will not enter the subjective world of the objective; instead, you will criticize and analyze it from the outside. It will probably also alienate the other, who, in turn, will not want to reveal private, personal, and intimate details of his subjective life.

However, by adopting the previous approach, that of connected knowledge, you will gain access to the subjective world of the objective because you will think and feel as if it were your subjective world. At the end of the day, you may not accept the thought of the objective; however, you will have succeeded in exploring the details of them and, therefore, will have reached a more enlightened perspective from which to analyze, criticize and offer advice.

Let's emphasize that separate and connected knowledge are methodological approaches to knowledge. As such, each one has value in its appropriate contexts. Separate knowledge uses techniques such as the devil's advocate and logical refutation.

5. *Use the reflection.*

Note that the last questions are open, which means they cannot be answered with a yes or no. Consequently, such questions facilitate dialogue and, therefore, help foster understanding. In addition, a device that can further promote empathic understanding is known as reflection.

First presented by the psychologist, Carl Rogers, as a way to express empathic understanding in the context of counseling, reflection implies trying to clarify what another person is saying by reflecting (not repeating) what an objective is thinking or feeling.

"It seems that you feel very disappointed that you have not received a raise," "It seems that you are thinking that others are judging you negatively when you are wrong." These questions not only help facilitate the development of the objective of your narrative but also demonstrate that you are listening to him; They also help to involve one as a partner in the exploration of the subjective life of the objective, thus promoting greater clarity and understanding of the narrative. This can increase the potential to "connect" and "enter" into this subjective world instead of seeing it from an external point of view.

6. *Listen to the objective.*

The reflection aims to improve the understanding of the objective (as well as the understanding of the person who is reflecting) by introducing deeper meanings and implications embedded in the narrative of the objective. It is good if you do that and poor if you do not add anything to what the objective has already said. So saying, "It seems you don't like your father" to someone who just said, "I hate that son of a bitch!" brings nothing to the table, either cognitively or emotionally.

At most, it is likely to be received with a "No, duh." In contrast, the answer: "It seems that you feel that your father was not there for you when you needed him" could open new avenues to expand the narrative. In fact, even if the reflection is wrong, it could help clarify things. But too many inaccurate reflexes can also destroy the prospects of empathizing with the goal.

Listening carefully to the narrative of the objective is therefore essential to produce useful reflections; because it is only through "active" listening (which includes asking open-ended questions as mentioned) that you are more likely to see within the subjective world to capture deeper meanings and implications of what the objective says.

Therefore, if you are in the habit of speaking or lecturing to others, instead of listening to them, you may not be empathetic, unless you make a concerted effort to overcome this habit.

7. *Use self-disclosure as appropriate.*

One way to not listen carefully is to spend time talking about yourself. In fact, others may not open up and share their private, subjective worlds if they have few opportunities to talk about themselves and think that you are more interested in yourself than in them.

However, self-disclosure can be a useful and powerful way to connect with shared values when it is relevant and not excessive. In fact, the self-revelation that your own subjective world brings in proximity to that of the objective can also adorn and improve empathy.

8. Adequately distance oneself from the subjective world of the objective.

Aristotle warned us to look for "the gold mean" between excess and deficiency in matters related to the passions. For example, moral virtues such as courage avoid extremes between cowardice and folly; friendship avoids the extremes of rudeness and flattery; and the temperance of insensitivity and complacency.

Similarly, as a moral virtue, empathy can be seen as an average between two extremes: being too far from the subjective world of the objective and too close to it. In fact, if you are worried about your own personal problems of life, then you are not likely to get close enough to the subjective world of the objective to identify with the objective of your problems.

On the other hand, if you get too personally involved in that subjective world, you will lose the Rogerian "as if," thus avoiding the distinction between you and the other. Therefore, the key to resonating with the subjective world of the objective is to avoid both extremes. Say you have been through a mess and are now listening to a friend who is going through a similar divorce.

If you start to see your friend's narrative as your own and start projecting your own emotions of anguish, then your friend's subjective world becomes yours; You no longer have any ability to constructively relate to your friend's plight because it is yours.

Then you get lost in that world, and you drown ineptly in it along with your friend. On the other hand, if you face the difficult situation of your friend with a cold "get over it" and, consequently, you fail to connect with your friend, you will be too far from your friend's subjective world to be very useful. So what is the right distance and how to get there?

9. *Practice it!*

Of course, when strong emotions come on, it is not always easy to apply such a filter, but that is precisely why empathy requires practice and perseverance to cultivate the right habit. It is also the reason why empathy is a virtue or excellence of being human.

Therefore, I urge you to practice applying these guidelines when a friend, a family member, a significant other, a colleague, a client, or another relation of yours only wants someone to talk to. Since it is not difficult to find such contexts in the mainstream of life, it is quite easy to find the opportunity to practice empathy.

The practice will not make you perfect because nobody is perfect, but it can, in fact, help make you more empathetic. And that, in turn, can be invaluable in improving the quality of their interpersonal relationships.

CHAPTER 6
WHAT IS CODEPENDENCY?

For quite some time, I have been engaged in psychotherapeutic work with people who have suffered love losses, call these divorces, separation, courtship, etc. Also, at the same time, I have worked with people who suffer from severe toxic or at least quite dysfunctional relationships, which means that they are related to couples who violate, aggravate, manipulate and destroy their emotional balance or, as we call it, in Psychology, your homeostasis.

Then, after observing repeated patterns of behavior, of listening—again and again— to the same stories of suffering and of noticing identical relationship dynamics, it is quite clear to me that these people share something more than simply maintaining a harmful relationship or suffering a lot from a terminated relationship. These people share something called Codependency.

I have always believed that this condition is the cancer of the emotional problems of a couple. Almost all other feelings and behaviors that assault a person when suffering from an unhealthy or dysfunctional relationship (jealousy, humiliation, violence, loss of self-esteem, etc.), are derived—directly or indirectly—from being codependent.

Codependency is a mental and emotional condition, that is, psychologically, that appears in someone who repeatedly shows excessive concern—and usually exaggerated—for others, for example, their partner.

Codependency is also called affective attachment because it is formed by the belief that without the person to whom I am attached and who takes care of me or who I take care of, my life does not make much sense. Therefore, codependency is a conflicting and addictive relationship with the other person.

I say that it is conflicting because it generates wrong ideas and behaviors that clash directly with what a good relationship is and also with the emotional stability of the people involved. The matter is complicated because it is also addictive. This type of relationship causes these wrong ideas and behaviors to be maintained regardless of the level of physical, mental, and emotional damage that we are suffering or generate in the other.

Codependency addiction has to do with two factors. First of all, there is the issue that in a codependent relationship, the thought that prevails is that of "getting away with it" by each of the members. And this works in a dynamic of "I give" and "I get." For this to happen, it is mandatory that in a codependent relationship, there are two types of codependents.

Codependent slave and rescuer

First, there is the "enslaving" codependent, which is the one we all relate to codependency: the one that depends on the other, that is, the one that enslaves the partner. But there is also one more that we do not usually consider as codependent, who is the "rescuer" or as I love to call them, codependent "ambulance." The one who is responsible for being enslaved by his/her partner for the sake of "saving him/her."

The second point that has to do with addiction in codependency is that both the "enslaving" and the "rescuer" codependent have two specific ways of obtaining profit from the other (although this gain is not—in reality—codependency).

The enslaving codependent deploys a mechanism of dominance over his partner using manipulation and, more specifically, his harmful part: emotional blackmail. That is, he enslaves the other through "If you do not do what I want, you will pay the consequences;" but he does not do it directly, but veiledly. Something like "Poor me, look at how I suffer because of you."

Meanwhile, the "ambulance" couple exercises such dominance over their partner more frontally than the "enslaver." And this is done through control. This type of codependent tries, by all means, to impose his will, his points of view, his way of behaving and feeling on the other. And this control is direct, usually based on mechanisms such as emotional, mental, and economic restrictions. More or less like "Why don't you do what I tell you? Don't you see what is best for you?

As you can see, this is the codependent mechanism in a couple, and although the couple in codependency has indeed moved from "rescuer" to "enslaver" and vice versa throughout the relationship, it is also true that one of the two permeates your personality more.

However, I also want to give you in this chapter, the seven characteristics that can tell you if you are codependent. These characteristics, as I told you at the beginning, are the product of observations, studies, and work with codependents of emotional and mental health professionals.

The characteristics that a codependent presents

Of course, the factors presented below are not decisive (use your assertiveness), but they are influential in the issue of codependency. These features are:

1. You grew up in a dysfunctional home (like all people, but the way in which they develop codependency is to the extent that dysfunctionality has passed) You probably lived with addicted parents who fought or were violent—not necessarily physical violence—all or most of the time. This violence in parents also occurs when they "loved each other and had no problems," but in the background there were behaviors such as ignoring the other, alcoholism, or infidelities.

2. No matter how hard you tried, you did not receive recognition from your parents. They were usually so involved in their neuroses that the last thing they did was pay attention to you.

3. This is one of my favorites. If you were an extremely mature girl or boy for your age, it was out of necessity since you had to grow fast to take care of your siblings, your parents, and even to survive. This "maturity" caused you to skip the healthy stages of your childhood or youth development.

4. You are unable to set limits because that would mean saying no to people, and since—according to you and your codependency—that means that those people stop loving, accepting or protecting you, you prefer to lower your head and accept things you don't want do, think or feel.

5. Another one of my favorites. Other people are always more important than you. Since you lived in a dysfunctional home, nobody used to listen to you unless you were useful for someone's purposes. In this way, you grew up with the conditioning of satisfying the needs of others to exchange it for love or acceptance.

6. You feel the excessive weakness of the weak, the oppressed, and those who suffer injustices (or at least what you consider injustices). Your thought is almost to consider yourself a superhero (remember the "ambulances"?).

7. Finally and paradoxically, you can't stand to be vulnerable because you think this is synonymous with weakness. This happens because, in your family of origin, the expression of your feelings was not allowed, and when it occurred, it was censored or seen as a defect.

As you can see, there is quite a lot of force in these signals, and I am sure that at this moment you may realize that you relate to several of them—if not all of them.

The good news is that codependency can be changed. You can stop being codependent if you want to. This is achieved based on hard work with a mental health professional and particularly the recognition and understanding you can begin to have about it.

Signs That You Are In A Codependency Relationship

Codependency is a psychological pathology in which one of the two individuals (or both) makes the other the center of their universe, becoming a "satellite" without a life of its own.

If some of the following signals sound very familiar to you, it is time to reflect on whether the level of codependency you have with your partner will end up destroying them both. The greater the number of accumulated symptoms, the greater the chances that the ending will not be happy.

You are one of those who say "Amen" to everything your partner suggests, even if it goes against your wishes.

According to the psychologist, Darlene Lancer, quoted in PsychCentral.com, it is not bad to try to please your loved one, cooking for him or letting him choose the movie you will see together, for example, but if you say NO to their requests or choices and you produce anxiety, then you are driving your tendency to please him on an unhealthy path.

You no longer think for yourself

And as a consequence, you have nothing to contribute in matters of big decisions, nor do you have a respected voice in the relationship.

In the opinion of psychologist, Nicole Martinez, Psy.D, LCPC, a clear sign of codependency is when one of the two begins to repeat in public what their partner believes on various topics, regardless of their own opinions and thoughts to engage in on the other.

You feel guilty about not being able to help your partner more and better

If your partner has a serious problem such as drug, alcohol, or sex addiction, you feel bad about not being able to help them out of their problem. And this is due, according to Shawn M. Burn, Ph.D. in Psychology Today, to one of the pillars of codependency which is the need to feel important to the other ... to know that the other needs you and that without you they cannot exist.

You experience high levels of anxiety

It is logical to assume that postponing the satisfaction of your own needs for a long time leads to experiencing anxiety in daily life. In an interview for The Sun, psychologist Seth Meyers argues that codependents experience anxiety more frequently than any other type of emotions and that they invest a lot of time and energy at two extremes: trying to change their partner or trying to become who their partner wants them to be, and this is exhausting.

Your limits are confusing

The codependency relationship leads you to abdicate your convictions. Recently I had two women with high levels of anxiety and depression in consultation because their husbands have been forcing them to practice the lifestyle of the swingers (who exchange sexual partners) against their will. And their justification has been that they wanted to please their husbands and that they were afraid of losing them by not doing so.

Your love is conditional

Most likely, you are in a codependent relationship because with it; you want to fill an existential void. For example, if you need to feel important, you enter into relationships with people who have neither stability nor emotional health, and you stay with them to see their change... what interests you is that they become who you think they should be ... You don't accept them for who they are. Your happiness depends on them being who you want them to be, and this is not good for you nor them.

You are jealous, possessive and controlling or your partner is, or both

You want to know and be part of everything your partner does. You don't miss anything or anyone. You want to be in control of all the situations related to your partner, and many times you get to deal with very personal issues such as clothes or the daily agenda.

You feel you don't deserve better and are afraid of loneliness

People stay in wrong relationships for all kinds of reasons. In the case of codependents, it is because they believe that they will not find anything better if they end the relationship they have at the moment. They look pessimistically at a future without that person who constantly hurts them and sometimes even blame themselves for their love drama.

Likewise, people immersed in a codependent relationship have a high fear of loneliness, and this is often the root of the problem. They cannot imagine life without a partner, so they cling sickly to what they have. Most likely, they have come from similar relationships in their past and will still have them in the future if they do not receive professional help.

If you think you are in a codependency relationship, don't die. For this, as for so many other problems in life, there are viable solutions at hand. Seek help together. But if your partner doesn't recognize any problem in the relationship, maybe it's time to let them go... for the good of both of you.

CHAPTER 7
UNDERSTANDING NARCISSISTS

A certain degree of narcissism has long been considered a prerequisite for a healthy self-image—one needs to be able to love oneself in order to love others. For people with a narcissistic personality disorder, however, these traits have become completely dominant and, instead, create major problems, not least in relation to others.

Narcissistic personality traits are relatively abundant in the population, but fully developed narcissistic personality disorders are not even considered one percent.

The dominant trait is an inflated self-image, where the person perceives himself as magnificent, exalted, and successful. Since the basis for the elevated self-image is very fragile, the person will also be very sensitive to criticism. In addition, there is also a marked lack of empathy.

Grandiosity and self-overestimation easily lead to loneliness and even depression because one cannot get the high thoughts about oneself confirmed by others.

People with narcissistic personality disorder have strikingly often antisocial or borderline traits, which further complicate the symptom picture and treatment.

Causes And Treatment

Narcissistic people do not tend to frequent inquiries from professional psychology and mental health, but it is quite common that some patients refer to problems following persons living with the narcissistic profile.

Does it always become a topic of conversation? Do you feel entitled to certain rights or privileges? Do you despise others? These are classic signs of a narcissistic personality disorder. Do you know someone who feels that he is always right and others are not? Is he arrogant, lacking empathy, and thinks he is very important? That person may have this disorder.

There are also people with Narcissistic Personality Disorder in many areas, and of course, also in public life or in the media.

What is narcissistic personality disorder?

This is a disorder that affects approximately 1% of the population with a higher prevalence in men than women. It is characterized by an exaggerated arrogance, lack of empathy, and a great need for admiration. The main marker of the narcissistic personality is grandiosity. They care about power, prestige, and vanity and believe they deserve special treatment.

Narcissistic personality disorder should not be confused with a person with high self-esteem. A person with high self-esteem can be humble, while the narcissist cannot. They are selfish, presumptuous, and ignore the feelings and needs of others. In addition, the disorder affects a person's life in a negative way. In general, the person may be unhappy with his life and disappointed when others do not admire him or give him special treatment or the attention he needs. All vital areas are affected (work, personal, social...), but the person is not able to realize that their behavior negatively affects their relationships. People are not comfortable with a narcissistic person, and they will be dissatisfied with their work, their social life, etc.

What are the causes of this type of disorder?

Although the causes of narcissistic personality disorder are not yet exact, many mental health professionals believe that it results from a combination of factors that may be related to:

- genetics - hereditary characteristics;
- environment - mismatches in relationships with caregivers in childhood (excessive dedication or excessive criticism);
- Neurobiology - the connection between thinking and behavior that involves temperament and the ability to manage tensions.

What characteristics help to identify the disorder?

Identifying a person with a narcissistic personality may be difficult, but several scientific studies point to some of the key features of this type of disorder. Check out some of them below.

- Irritation and nervousness when contradicted

Narcissistic individuals are hypersensitive to criticism and insults (real or imagined) and cannot handle defeats, frustrations, and rejections well—

so they have no emotional maturity. Thus, when contradicted, they may react with anger, irritation, and nervousness. Because they have low self-esteem, they use aggression to disguise their insecurity.

- An exaggerated sense of superiority and importance

Those suffering from a narcissistic disorder believe that their priorities, interests, and opinions are more important and more valuable than anyone else's. Their perception and speech are always focused on overemphasizing their "importance." A smug view of themselves is one of the main ways in which narcissists gives themselves permission to control and dominate others.

- The belief of being special and unique

The narcissist's belief that he is special, unique and can only be understood by other special people is an idea that is part of a survival mechanism that helps him face the world. They are often defined by what they consider their exceptional qualities—and as soon as we know them, they warn us about them.

- Lack of empathy

The narcissist usually has no empathy; that is, he is unable to put himself in the shoes of others and to express compassion in the face of the suffering of others. His problems, pain, and point of view dominate the universe. Nothing reflects the behavior of the narcissistic individual so much as the inability to understand and identify with the experience of others.

- They are manipulators

Narcissists like to manipulate people, especially since they believe that others are only there to satisfy their desires and needs. Therefore, they are considered manipulation artists.

Narcissistic Personality Disorder Symptoms

Patients with narcissistic personality disorder are very sensitive to heartache from criticism or defeat. They often do not demonstrate this and begin to feel humiliated, degraded, and empty. In some cases, the reaction may be disdain, anger or aggressive counterattack.

Sometimes these experiences generate a social detachment or enormous effort to be humble in order to hide the grandeur. Interpersonal relationships are typically compromised by problems arising from presumption, the need for admiration, and the relative disregard for the sensitivity of others. While ambition and trust can lead to high achievements, performance can be disrupted by intolerance of criticism or defeat.

Another important aspect is that these patients, despite having an injury, often have high financial conditions and good positions, not being in presence of labor difficulties.

A woman with the narcissistic disorder, like all narcissistic people, does things just because she thinks she will make a profit.

But the big differences between a narcissistic man and woman are that women are overly concerned with their social status, so they use sex to achieve their goals and their way of manipulating is much more subtle than that of a narcissistic man.

The narcissistic woman complies with the features described in the DSM-5 that you have seen at the point of narcissistic personality disorder, but they also have very specific characteristics.

CHAPTER 8
TYPES OF NARCISSISTS

1. Emotional dependent narcissist

This type of narcissism is characterized by an extreme "vulnerability." This narcissistic person experiences an enormous need for love, and is not satisfied with anything. It's like a bottomless pit that never fills. He simply believes that he does not receive enough love, he feels fleetingly satisfied with the attention of others, but then he experiences that emptiness of approval and affection again. At the base of this behavior lies a deep fear of rejection and abandonment, so the narcissist clings to dependence. To meet those needs, he has no qualms with manipulating others. His emotional demands are growing, so his partner and close people drain emotionally to try to nurture, comfort and sustain that "I" so in need of affection.

2. Classic Narcissism

It encompasses the typical features of common narcissism, says exhibitionism, the sense of superiority, and the high degree of functionality in general aspects.

Their egocentric behavior betrays them, usually having conversations with other people about themselves or their different achievements, showing a clear dislike when the issues are not of personal interest.

Despite their marked sense of superiority to others, they need the recognition of other people to feed their ego, due to the low self-esteem they hide.

3. Vulnerable Narcissist

Also known as Closet Narcissist, they stand out because, despite their marked sense of superiority to others, their shyness makes them refuse to be the center of attention even when the occasion warrants. They tend to be more fragile to the criticisms or opinions of others, in addition to preferring to get together with people who receive admiration than to receive admiration themselves.

A characteristic fact in this type of narcissist is their false sense of altruism, in which they demonstrate great compassion or excessive generosity, only to compensate for the guilt caused by their disinterest in others.

4. Evil Narcissist

Also called Toxic Narcissist, is characterized by being highly manipulative and inconsiderate of situations beyond their interest. They also show serious antisocial traits, uncommon in the other two types of narcissism, in relation to sociopathy and psychopathy.

Their objective is to possess the power and control over others, reaching to manifest high-risk behaviors until they achieve their mission, without demonstrating any remorse and, in some cases, getting to enjoy their actions.

Other Subtypes of Narcissism

As for less obvious characteristics, there are also certain identifiable features in narcissists who relate with one group over another. These might be:

1. Narcissist Open vs. Narcissist Undercover

This classification is related to the behavior used by the narcissist to ensure that their objectives are met, the former being a passive-aggressive form while the latter a more covert.

That is, the Open Narcissist can manipulate people frontally to do what he wants, while the Undercover Narcissist is usually more discreet and with more complex plans.

Following this idea, Classic Narcissists are classified as Open Narcissists, while Vulnerable Narcissists do so with Undercover Narcissism. The Evil Narcissist can be classified as both as the case may be.

2. Somatic Narcissist vs. Brain Narcissist

They they usually show greater pride when they relate to others and this can be a physical attraction or a characteristic of their personality.

Its classification among the 3 main types of narcissism will depend on the case since anyone can show the features of this subtype.

3. Inverted Narcissist

This subtype only relates to the Vulnerable Narcissist, being a characteristic in which he seeks to relate to other narcissists to feel in some way special.

They are the only narcissists who develop codependency traits with other people, instead of manipulating the people around them until they become codependent to them.

As you may have seen, there are characteristics that make a marked difference between one narcissist and another, to the point of considering adaptive to some and dangerous to others.

There are other faces of narcissism. Even people who spend a lot of time on their appearance can be narcissists. The social networks, with their flattering comments about their appearance, strengthen the narcissistic streak of these people. In addition, they may believe that they, due to their appearance, deserve to get everything, such as, a partner or a specific job.

Then there are other types of narcissists who consider themselves messianic beings whose wisdom is infinite. This only reinforces the sense of superiority (or weakens the sense of inferiority). This type of narcissist "helps" others, even if they do not ask for it. In this way, they try to score points with others to later ask of them a favor.

Then there are narcissists who boast successes and accomplishments that they have never really achieved, at least not in the way they tell their story. With that, they want to arouse others' admiration. However, the admiration of their fellow human beings often turns into the opposite as soon as they realize that these were only false stories. At this point, they are already telling a new lie.

CHAPTER 9
NARCISSIST MANIPULATION TECHNIQUES

- **Cycle: idealization-devaluation-abandonment**

This involves a sudden transition from a fairytale love story, treating you like an ideal, to subtle comments and constant criticism, often hidden, negating the legitimacy of your needs or preferences. In the idealization phase, you begin to feel that you have never felt like this before and are as if on an emotional high.

A relationship with a narcissist is like a drug addiction. At first, it is great, and then the narcissist takes away your drug supply, i.e., your attention and feelings become withdrawn for no apparent reason. It starts to give you less and less, expecting more and more.

You will do everything to have at least a bit of the man he was (or rather, the man he was pretending to be) at the very beginning of the relationship. When the mask begins to fall, and you begin to orient yourself to where you are, very often abandonment occurs.

Abandonment does not necessarily mean the end of the relationship, it is often a total physical and emotional withdrawal; ignoring you, the so-called silent treatment (quiet days). Some narcissists at this stage give up completely, entering into another relationship, which they often begin while still with you.

Very often, abandonment, offending at amen is also a reaction of narcissistic personalities to the opposition, to setting boundaries or paying attention to their unacceptable behavior.

This mechanism is not only found in romantic relationships, but also in other relationships.

Narcissism often makes us feel guilty about this method of manipulation. This is to divert attention from his behavior and make us focus on our REACTION and feel guilty that, e.g., we reacted badly, too violently; we chose the wrong words, etc. The truth is that dysfunctional narcissistic behavior is the problem, not your reaction to it. After narcissistic abandonment, the victim often feels worthless, drained of energy, lost and totally confused.

- **Gaslighting**

Is a technique used by violent people to convince you that there is something wrong with your perception. Narcissists will convince you that you perceive reality incorrectly and may even tag you with mental illness. In extreme cases, they can even store items at home and convince you that you did it. As a result of gaslighting, the victim ceases to trust himself, his feelings, and he stops listening to intuition, he stops believing that what he sees and experiences is real. Gaslighting makes you start questioning yourself and believing that maybe something is wrong with you.

- **Smear campaigns (slander)**

Narcissists often hold up a whole harem of potential victims. These can be contacts to former partners or, e.g., an account on a dating site. Very often, they can be with you and simultaneously smear you behind your back to your potential goals or to family members/friends, etc. Of course, you do not know it. Very often, a narcissist outside the house is a charming, almost flawless man. He tries to keep a circle of people who worship him or are just like him. Be prepared to always be perceived as bad/angry in his circle and no one will believe you regarding what happened behind closed doors. You will be presented as a madwoman.

- **Triangulation**

Deliberately causing jealousy, lack of stability and security by talking about your former partners, keeping in touch with them, and comparing yourself to others. It can also be a deliberate placement of photos or items belonging to former partners or potential partners (e.g., friends) so that they are found. It evokes the feeling that there is still a third person in the relationship. Often, the narcissist's partner also begins to play detective because of the growing lack of trust.

- **Two faces (or more)**

You can't comprehend how it is possible that one person can be great one moment, and behave as if you were enemy No. 1 the next moment. You don't know what to expect, you tiptoe, live like a ticking bomb. Stress becomes an integral part of your everyday life. Outside, your partner praises you to the heavens and arranges hell for you at home. In the evening, he launches a real brawl for a trivial reason, and in the morning he acts as if nothing ever happened: "What are we doing today?" or "What's for breakfast?". It puts you in total confusion, you feel like you are in a fog, you no longer know what is true and what is not, with whom are you actually in a relationship? Who is this? You can't define this man because he changes his face as often as he likes depending on the situation.

Signs of a Narcissist Person

- **Admiration**

Narcissists dominate the conversation. They like to talk about themselves, their exploits, and sometimes alter the truth by exaggerating their exploits. They give advice even when nobody asks them, and they feel superior to others. Nothing frustrates them more than waiting, and they believe that their needs should be considered a priority by their entourage, or even by society as a whole.

- **The Ambition**

Wanting to advance in his career and/or his private life is quite natural, but narcissists are much more ambitious than the rest of the population, says the site, Health. They tend to believe that they are part of an elite that deserves only the best and that a bright future awaits them. For them, people are either winners or losers, and it goes without saying that they surround themselves only with the first ones.

- **Manipulation**

Despite their characteristics as described above, narcissists are sometimes difficult to identify because they know how to charm their entourage.

They manage to make others feel important. But at the slightest criticism against them, everything is destroyed. They cannot stand to receive judgments and tend to use their manipulative skills to get what they want or need. In question, explain the specialists cited by Health, a lack of deep empathy.

- **The Grudge**

Despite a very apparent self-confidence, narcissists are not indifferent to others. That is why, from the first signs of disapproval, they feel personally attacked. This injury will cause a lot of anger, grudges, and, in some cases, a desire for revenge. This problematic situation is compounded by the fact that narcissists refuse to be held responsible for their mistakes or bad behavior and tend to accuse others in their place.

CHAPTER 10
NARCISSISM IN RELATIONSHIP

Narcissists are usually unable to maintain a healthy relationship. Many have a turbulent history of relationships, and a lot of emotional baggage. They take, they ask, they expect. In return, they give very little, except beautiful words.

American research conducted at the University of Georgia recently revealed that narcissists are poor in relationships. Researchers concluded that while narcissists appear charming and full of self-confidence, they can quickly engage all sorts of people, but at the same time, they rarely succeed in building a long-term relationship. From the information provided by the narcissists themselves and also from the stories of their current and former partners, she concluded that narcissists are self-centered, manipulative, unfaithful, and power-hungry in relationships. The love style of narcissists is, therefore 'game-playing-love': they want to be the boss, keep their distance, often cheat and do everything they can to not become dependent on their partner.

Signs Of Narcissism In Relationship

The narcissist is someone who "buried his true self-expression in relation to some past trauma and replaced it with a highly developed and compensatory false version of himself."

- This alternate personality usually wants to show that he is grand, "above all," and highly pretentious.
- In our highly individualistic society, mild and severe forms of narcissism are widespread.
- Narcissism is often interpreted in popular culture as a self-loving person.
- It is more accurate to characterize the pathological narcissist as someone who is in love with the idealized self-image that one designs to avoid (and be seen as) the real, wounded, selfless version.
- Deep down, most pathological narcissists feel like the "ugly duckling," even though they don't want to admit it.

How To Tell If You're Dating A Narcissist?

Although most of us are blamed for some of the behaviors below from time to time, the pathological narcissist tends to permanently touch these varied personalities while still not knowing how their actions affect other people.

- **The Owner of the Conversation.**

The narcissist loves to talk about himself and doesn't give you a chance to get in the conversation.

You have trouble being heard, and you can't share your opinions and feelings.

When you finally get a word out, if you don't agree with the narcissist, your comments will probably be corrected, dismissed, or ignored.

"My boyfriend's favorite answers to my opinions are always: "but...," " actually..." and "it's so much more than just that..." He always has to think he knows more. - **anonymous.**

- **The Chat Switch.**

While many people have a bad habit of interrupting others during a conversation, the narcissist quickly interrupts and shifts the focus back to him. He shows little genuine interest in you.

- **The Rules Breaker.**

The narcissist likes to violate social rules and norms, such as breaking the line, stealing small objects, missing an appointment, or disobeying traffic laws.

- **The Bound Violator.**

Shows wide disrespect for other people's thoughts, feelings, belongings, and physical space.

He uses other people without consideration or sensitivity.

He takes and borrows your money and doesn't return it.

He breaks promises and obligations repeatedly.

He shows little remorse and blames the victim for her own lack of respect for herself.

"It's your fault that I forgot why you didn't warn me." - **anonymous.**

- **False Self Image Projection.**

Many narcissists like to do things to impress others when they want to look good externally.

This trophy complex can appear in physical, romantic, sexual, social, religious, financial, material, professional, academic, or cultural aspects.

In these situations, the narcissist uses people, objects, status, or achievements to represent his self-image, replacing the actual but inadequate image.

These merits are often exaggerated.

The subliminal message of this kind of show is, "I am better than you!" Or "Look how special I am—I am worthy of everyone's love and acceptance!"

"I dyed my hair blonde and put on silicone to get men's attention—and make other women jealous."

"My achievements are everything."

"I will never want to pass myself off as a poor person. My fiancée and I drove a new BMW. A groomsman for our wedding also has a BMW."

These external symbols eventually become part of the narcissist's false identity, replacing the person's actual and hurt version.

- **What Is In The Law Of Everything?**

Narcissists often expect preferential treatment from others.

They expect other people to meet their needs, often instantly, without considering the person in return.

In this narcissistic mindset, the world revolves around him.

- **The Charming.**

Narcissists can be very charismatic and persuasive.

When they are interested in you (to their own gratification), they make you feel very special and dear.

However, once they lose interest in you (most likely after getting what they wanted... or getting sick), they may walk away from you without thinking twice.

The narcissist can be very engaging and sociable as long as you are fulfilling what he wants and giving him your full attention.

- **Great Personality.**

Thinking of yourself as a hero, prince, or some extremely special person.

Some narcissists have an exaggerated sense of self-importance, believing that other people cannot live or survive without their magnificent contribution.

"Once again, I saved the day—they are nothing without me."

- **Negative Emotions.**

Many narcissists like to raise and spread negative emotions to gain attention, to feel the power, and to make you insecure and unbalanced.

They are easily irritated by any sign of inattention, real or perceived.

The narcissist can make a scene if you disdain his opinions or fail to meet his expectations.

Narcissists are extremely sensitive to criticism, usually, react with heated arguments (fight), or move away and get cold (escape).

On the other hand, narcissists are quick to judge, criticize, ridicule, and blame you.

- **Manipulation: Using Other People As An Extension Of Yourself.**

Make decisions for others to meet their own needs.

The narcissist can use his or her romantic partner, a child, friend, or colleague to fulfill an unreasonable need, fulfil unrealized dreams, or cover self-perceived defects.

"If my son doesn't become a successful professional soccer player, I will defeat him."

Another way narcissists manipulate is through guilt, such as saying things like "I gave myself out so much, and you are so ungrateful," or "I am the victim here—you have to help me, otherwise you are not a good person."

They hijack your emotions and force you to make sacrifices that are beyond your means.

If you're in a relationship with a difficult-to-deal narcissist, be more proactive rather than reactive... and know how to say no to his over-requests.

Tips To Live With A Narcissistic Person

Loving a narcissist can be as rewarding as it is difficult. Here are some techniques to ask the right questions and improve the life of a couple.

If you like a narcissistic person, whether it's an official diagnosis or a simple interest in his own belly button, you may be wondering if you are self-destructive or masochistic. Still, loving a narcissist can be as rewarding as it is difficult, say experts at Psychology Today. There is no way to know in advance if the relationship will work or not, but there are tips to ensure certain well-being to the couple.

- **Listen**

No matter what you've heard or read, narcissists can be charming. If your relationship satisfies you most of the time, you can ignore your surroundings. But if you constantly complain to your partner or your loved ones, it is likely that you will not listen. It's even a sign that the relationship is not good for you, but it's difficult to listen to others when that's the case. So open your ears when you talk to others about your relationship, you may be surprised by your own remarks.

• Ask Yourself The Right Questions

Sometimes we stay in a relationship with a narcissist because it makes us feel special in the eyes of others. If your entourage admires your partner, you may enjoy this type of "power" and prestige. But ask yourself honestly if what the relationship brings you is worth staying for.

• Strengthen the positive

Researchers have found that praising a particular behavior, such as how to handle a certain situation, or making someone happy, reinforces the behavior in question. According to Psychology Today, you can promote your partner's self-esteem in the event of a problem.

• Practice mindfulness

The practice of mindfulness would help some people with narcissism to live better. This type of meditation makes it possible, for example, to recognize anger and to change its behavior before it degenerates. If you want to offer this activity smoothly, without rushing your partner, you can start by practicing it yourself, then invite him to try it.

- **To be realistic**

It is reasonable to expect that a specific behavior will improve, depending on the behavior, but it is not possible to expect a change of personality. So be realistic and ask yourself the right questions.

You can make a list of what you love about your partner and what you do not like, then ask yourself: Do the things I like make up for the things I do not like? Can I live long-term with the things I do not like? While some aspects of the relationship may change over time, others may never change.

What A Narcissistic Man Has During A Relationship

It may be the first time you hear the word "narcissistic," but perhaps you have lived with one for a long time. Could it be that you are in a relationship with a narcissistic man?

According to Greek mythology, Narcissus was a young man of great beauty that all women fell in love with; however, he rejected them. Nemesis, the goddess of revenge, seeing such abuse, punished him, making him fall in love with his own reflection in a lake. The attraction was so strong that Narcissus threw himself into the water and died there. From this legend comes the word "narcissist," referring to someone who only knows how to love himself.

Living with a person who has this pathology is very difficult. There are certain points that highlight whether someone is narcissistic or only has very high self-esteem. So you know how to distinguish if your partner has this problem or not, do not stop reading the following.

They have high self-esteem and give more importance than they have

Narcissists believe that the world will collapse if they are not there or at least make other people think that. Usually, in a conversation, a narcissist talks about how much he spent, who he talked to, what he did, but he will rarely talk about you and anything related to you.

These are vain and pretentious people who want the world to revolve around them.

Lacks empathy

When the person is not moved by the misfortune of others, we are in the presence of a narcissist. This type of person despises the rest because, in this way, he feels better about himself, although, in reality, the problem is that he has a great feeling of inferiority.

Does not support criticism

A narcissistic person does not support any criticism of his person. Instead of taking any suggestion towards something that he does like a good option to improve, he takes it as an insult and ends up misrepresenting everything by making the other feel guilty for something he did not do.

Narcissistic characteristics in women

Statistically, 75% of narcissists are men, and in general, the differences between their behaviors are small. But in the manifestation of narcissism, there are some differences because they emphasize different things. For example, men usually emphasize intellect, power, aggression, money, or social status. Women tend to emphasize the body, looks, charm, sexuality, female household "traits" or their children.

Narcissistic women assert themselves with their body and may even manifest anorexia, nervosa or bulimia. Or they flaunt and exploit their physical charms, their sexuality, and their social and cultural life by affirming their 'femininity.' They guarantee their source of worship through their more traditional gender roles, home to children, careers, suitability, their husbands, their feminine traits, and their role in society, etc.

Another difference is the way they react to treatment. Women are more likely to be involved in therapy because, as a rule, women are more likely to admit their psychological problems. Men are a little less inclined to publicize their problems (due to rooted machismo)—it does not necessarily mean that they are less likely to admit to themselves their emotional conflicts.

The general rule of the narcissistic person cannot be forgotten: the narcissist uses everything around him to obtain his (or her) source of narcissistic idolatry. As a rule in women, this source becomes a child because of the way our society is still structured and the fact that women are still the only ones giving birth. It is easier for women to think of their children as their extension because since they were actually their physical extensions as they were connected in the womb, there was a more intense and extensive interaction.

The narcissistic woman respects her children as significant sources for her ego, while the male narcissist is more likely to regard his children as a nuisance rather than as a source of gratification and supply. As we still live in a society of inequality, men have many narcissistic sources for their egos, while women struggle to maintain their most reliable source of supply, their children. So she starts early on an insidious indoctrination, guilt, emotional sanctions, deprivation, and other psychological mechanisms; she tries to induce a dependence on them that cannot be easily broken. There is no difference in behavioral psychodynamics between the male and female narcissists, but there is a difference in their narcissistic source choices.

The narcissistic woman exercises the same control technique as the narcissistic man, is emotionally abusive, master of "control" through verbal force, keen thinking, and emotional blackmail. Such people cling to their belief system, no matter how many times they are confronted with contrary evidence, however wrong they may be, the more drama and indignation they may exhibit.

Here are some common control tactics of a narcissistic woman

- The narcissistic woman begins a conversation or attack with a topic.

When you start presenting facts that are contrary to your beliefs, however sincere they may be to you, you are never right. She goes off tangent, changes the subject, or makes a new accusation. While you are still defending your original point of view, she has already taken from her hat another series of problems, blame, and topics that may even be completely unrelated.

- She says, shut up! In explaining your feelings or point of view, this type of woman can brutally tell you to stop. "Shut up!" The narcissist cannot handle the truth, and they make an effort to deny and destroy the other person.
- Curses! This is the last resort of narcissists and other bullies. If they cannot defend their position or behaviors, they resort to emotion-based personal attacks. It's another distraction technique that deviates from the original point of the dispute by putting it on the defensive.
- Projection! They accuse and hold their victims responsible for actions or thoughts they have caused and are guilty of. This is a primitive defense mechanism. For example, I once heard a

mother blaming her daughter for the birthday parties she had to hold in childhood.

- Division! The narcissist sees the world as if it were all or nothing, right against evil, black and white. She has little ability to understand context or nuance. Either you see things her way, or you must be invalidated. You cannot agree and disagree with this kind of woman. Any criticism, the difference of opinion, or challenge to her authority is seen as a threat, and you will be treated in a way that will be devalued and demonized. This is the other primitive defense mechanism.
- Prepare and attack! For a narcissist, discord or contempt is not enough. Everyone else in your world, including your own family and friends, should be hated and defeated for being wrong.
- Gaslighting! Women using this tactic to deny things they have said and done (and often the victim of the same transgressions they have committed). They distort reality by stating that the event never happened ... (you wondered ... you must be crazy) until you begin to doubt your own sanity ...

- Screams! There is no logic! With the narcissistic and emotionally abusive woman, the more wrong she is, the more she will raise her voice or the more stubborn she becomes. Her level of false indignation, revenge, and emotional withdrawal is in direct proportion to the way she faces you. She goes up, screaming, repeating the same simplistic, and emotionally-charged statements until she drowns out the reason, or simply withdraws in ignorance until you send an apology for your "crime."
- Guilt and shame! The narcissist blames others for all that is wrong in his life and never considers how he himself contributed to the situation or what his responsibility was, including whether or not they are unhappy, or it was never their fault ... there is always someone to blame. They transfer the responsibility to make you look bad or crazy, still making an effort to make you embarrassed and guilty in the end.
- They are unloading on the victim. When the narcissistic woman is placed against the wall or her dishonesty comes to light and she cannot deny it, she turns around

and throws the justification and responsibility of her conduct on the victim. Narcissistic women claim that they have only reacted to aggression and are being unfairly attacked, so they have acted in "self-defense" because they always stand up for the truth, and are the most honest, brave, and integral. They are practically illuminated!

CHAPTER 11
HOW TO DEAL WITH NARCISSISTS

Narcissistic attitudes can turn into a real nightmare for the people around you. Dealing with narcissists is not easy. They inflate their egos extremely. At the same time, they are as vulnerable as children. They have a lot of anxiety and inferiority.

People with a narcissistic attitude are very dependent on others' opinions. They feel better only if they get clear signs of praise and approval. But when they get criticized, they quickly collapse. The way people react is very different. Some may explode in anger and become aggressive. Or they may explode in their heart and become quiet.

This type of person may have a big ego. For narcissists, everything starts and ends with the ego. It's really hard for them to feel true empathy. That doesn't mean they are completely indifferent. They simply consider themselves the most important and cannot put others before themselves. They feel that they are unique.

The question is how we can deal with such people. Here are some suggestions.

- **Narcissists are very sensitive**

Don't forget this concept: Someone has a narcissistic attitude because he tries to add value to himself. In fact, they are worried that they may not be worth it. Just as a peacock looks threatening when it spreads its tail, yet it's actually scared. The only thing they are proud of is expressing the internal conflict that they cannot solve.

So they are very sensitive to criticism and indifference. You need to be very careful when talking to a narcissist. They are easily hurt. And it exacerbates their problems. They always want praise, but they should be praised only when appropriate.

Criticism should be expressed delicately and honestly. It is also important to clarify that you are not criticizing their confidence but criticizing their behavior.

Even if they don't look like that, they are hiding and suffering. They are likely to have had serious trauma in the past. They are just trying to live an experience that is not fully digested.

- **Don't let them manipulate you**

A narcissist may also be operational. If anything, they try to make others think the same way. Then people around them will say what they want to hear. In short, they reinforce the thoughts they want to believe.

They may be very good at it. They try to show how wonderful they are, and may be able to persuade you see them as intelligent and attractive.

Unfortunately, this kind of person may also underestimate the people around them. Because this helps maintain the illusion that they are better than their surroundings. They will look for ways to disqualify you or minimize your achievements. If it is a loved one, let them understand how they feel because of their actions.

What a narcissistic person needs is to believe in himself more. It is to feel true self-love. If they love themselves, they can feel important without inflating their egos. On the other hand, if the people around them try to manipulate them, their attitude will be stronger.

- **Don't be afraid to say no**

Narcissists like to use fear against you in any way possible.

They will find everything you fear and force you to live it. It's important that you face these fears, don't let them have that kind of control over you, and tell them that you're not afraid of them.

Free your past mistakes

Narcissists like to remember things that happened a long time ago so that you feel extremely bad about yourself once again. It is important that you recognize that you are only human, and everyone makes mistakes.

Forgive yourself for past mistakes; don't let them control the part of you that you've been working so hard on.

They will take advantage of your emotions whenever they can.

- **Change the subject**

Narcissists like to change the subject when they feel they are being attacked by someone.

When they are drawing your attention to the things they have done wrong, they will do everything in their power to try to change the subject in the hope that you will totally forget the problem.

- **Always feel free to say no**

The most important thing to remember when dealing with a narcissistic person is that you can always say no to anything you feel uncomfortable doing.

This will save you a lot of time and effort, and you will feel much better, saying no.

CHAPTER 12
NARCISSISTS AT WORK

A working environment characterized by tension, anxiety, criticism, low productivity... The narcissists at work undermine beneficial dynamics, initiatives, and even the simplest activities. They are people who must always be at the center of attention and achieve their merits through a fundamental and destructive strategy: to sabotage the rights and well-being of others.

Experts in the field of personality psychology show us that all of us, at some point in our lives, have narcissistic traits. But if a colleague, the boss, or someone else from our work context is in such a narcissistic phase, the situation can be as complicated as it is exhausting for us.

Keep in mind that the time we spend at work makes up most of our day. To do this, we need to add to the economic factor, the productive factor and the personal projection that we want to translate into our careers or within a company. Therefore, having to work with a person who radiates a harmful and toxic presence may cause all of these claims to be significantly reduced.

"Surrounding yourself with mediocre people is tantamount to surrounding yourself with toxic people, without noticing that the poisoned air is entering your pores and making you sick."

- Bernardo Stamateas

It is not easy to be surrounded by narcissists every day. Their behavior is often as irrational as it is exhausting, and unless we find strategies to defend ourselves, it can severely limit our quality of life. While there are studies, such as those conducted by the University of Illinois and published in the journal of Psychological Science, which indicate that the incidence of narcissistic personality has decreased in recent years, they remain a fact we cannot ignore.

It is important to know how we can deal with those people who are already in our lives, who do not succumb to anything or anyone, who do not give in, who want us to lose everything: the narcissists.

How to recognize them?

Those narcissists that you find in the workplace are known by many different names. It's the climbers, parasites, those who spread rumors, egoists, those who do not know how to work in a team, and those who make individual decisions without discussing them with anyone else. They are essentially those who create a stifling and unproductive climate that negates our motivation, initiative, and desire to go to work every morning.

There is also another aspect that should be understood with regard to narcissists. There are people who show a slightly different form of narcissistic traits. In fact, only a few fall into the small percentage of the population that actually suffers from a significant narcissistic personality disorder. So there are a few hardship cases, while others tend to become more affable and even change their behavior when given a reminder.

Let's see how these typically narcissistic people behave at work.

- They always want to be the focus.
- They want to claim the glory of shared services on their own.
- They would never admit that others did something right.
- They do not hesitate to show others and mock them.
- They use lies to achieve what they want.
- They sabotage the work of their colleagues.

- They take no responsibility for their own mistakes; they even manage to hold others responsible for them and point out their incompetence.
- We are dealing here with a very envious personality.
- They often urge other people to do unethical things.

In a study published by psychologists, Sander Thomas and Bram Bushman, of the University of Utrecht (The Netherlands), it is further noted that it is very common for us to first become enthusiastic about this narcissistic person. They can be both our boss, as well as the accessible, assertive and pleasant colleague with whom we get along very well in the beginning. But over time, their true intentions become apparent.

How do you survive narcissists at work?

Narcissists at work can make us feel burned out and exhausted and lose our hopes for working life. The problem becomes even more complex if the narcissistic person is our supervisor or boss, who believes he stands above his co-worker. Therefore, it is always advisable, especially if such a situation threatens to become active, to ask for labor law assistance.

On the other hand, one should make certain aspects clear. These are basic dimensions that can help us not to lose our motivation and goals.

Get to know the narcissist and his weaknesses

The first key is very simple: avoid getting involved in the narcissistic game. Therefore, it is very interesting to know that what such people need most is admiration and recognition. Their weak point is clearly their self-esteem; we must never forget that. Therefore, it is helpful to consider the following aspects:

- A narcissist always demands immediate attention: he feeds on it. It's best you do not give it to him.
- Let him see that his presence is secondary to you. Your priority is your work—to progress in your work and your goals.
- If the narcissist is your supervisor, you should avoid meeting his demands immediately, especially if they are not relevant, and your boss just wants to ridicule you.

Your needs have priority

The narcissist demands, humiliates, lies, pays attention only to himself, and sees nothing of his environment, except himself. Given this behavior, we must try to consistently enforce our needs and rights.

If something does not seem right to us, then we should speak out, especially when the other person speaks of himself in the first person and thus clearly shows their lack of empathy. But we must not be caught in their crushing web.

Everything in writing

Narcissists practice only one task at work, as we already know: exploiting others. Therefore, it is best to put any complaint in writing, whether by e-mail, mail, etc. If at any time, conflicting information appears or a special circumstance arises, we must be able to prove where this order came from and how we received it.

Do not tap into his traps

The narcissist wishes to know more and more about us in order to use his knowledge against us and in his favor. It also happens very often that at the beginning, he seeks our closeness to establish a kind of complicity and get information. We need to avoid falling into their traps and talking to them about personal matters, and we should be careful not to share any information or opinions with this kind of people as they could use them against us at any time.

Be aware of your strengths and rights in the workplace

One of the most common problems with such personalities is the complete lack of ethics. These people sabotage the rights of others, and what is worse, can even make them do illegal things.

That is why it is important that we always remember what our personal values are and that we are well informed about our employment situation. Narcissistic managers, for example, know how to wrap their vice and employees around them using unethical and sometimes illegal means to achieve their goals. Let us, therefore, avoid such situations, because we can prevent them from being more assertive by always remembering where our limits lie.

CHAPTER 13
WHAT IS EMOTIONAL INTELLIGENCE

Emotional intelligence (EQ) is the ability of a person to recognize and name their own and someone else's emotional states. It also includes dealing with one's own and other people's emotions, and is a very important and desirable social competence.

Emotional intelligence is part of the intelligence quotient, also known as IQ. It includes three levels. The first of these is the awareness of one's own emotions and the emotions of others. Level two is an important ability to manage emotions, e.g., calming down in a stressful situation. This is a very important and valuable skill, desirable in many situations. The third area of emotional intelligence is the ability to use emotions in problem-solving situations, e.g., using empathy in conflict situations and finding a compromise solution.

A person with a high level of emotional intelligence has the ability to make so-called insight into himself. This means that he can see the relationship between his emotions and his behavior and well-being, e.g., trembling hands in a situation of nervousness.

Emotional intelligence and its models

Emotional intelligence is a very important element of human personality equipment. This ability allows us to work on emotions, that is, recognizing them. How would we function without the ability to name what we feel? Interestingly, the lack of feeling emotions is called emotional illiteracy or alexithymia.

We also distinguish three models of emotional intelligence. The first of them assumes that emotional intelligence is the ability to understand one's emotions, thanks to which we can direct and control them and the ability to empathize with others. The author of this concept is the well-known psychologist, Daniel Goleman, author of many valuable publications on emotional intelligence. Another model includes a thesis on four areas that make up emotional intelligence. They are: perceiving emotions, understanding them, thinking supported by emotions, and the ability to manage emotions. Another model, in turn, changes these areas and adds another. These are inter- and intrapersonal intelligence, mood, adaptation to a new situation, and the ability to cope with stress.

Emotional Intelligence and Its Components

Emotional intelligence consists of two basic components. The first is psychological competence, i.e., relationships with oneself. They include self-esteem, self-awareness, and self-control. Self-esteem is nothing more than self-confidence. It is also being aware of your limitations and disadvantages. Self-awareness is already about emotions and includes recognizing your own emotional states and knowingly experiencing them. Self-control, in turn, is the ability to control your emotions and the ability to cope with stress.

The second component is social competence, relating to relations with the environment. They include five very important abilities. The first is empathy, the most important in understanding emotional intelligence. It means the ability to empathize with other people's emotional states. Another ingredient is persuasion, i.e., the ability to arouse in others desired emotional states or reactions, used, among others, in advertising. Assertiveness is another ability, i.e., the ability to defend one's own opinion without criticizing the position of others. Ability is cooperation, consisting in establishing contacts, creating relationships with people and cooperating with them in achieving a specific goal. The last ability is leadership, i.e., the ability to lead others and motivate them to act.

Many experts also include skill in acting as emotional intelligence. They include adaptive skills, diligence in action and motivation, i.e., commitment to action.

As you can see, emotional intelligence is a multidimensional construct, which means that it includes many factors or modules, as the above models show us. This also translates into its usability.

What Does Emotional Intelligence Consist Of?

Emotional intelligence consists of three basic competences, i.e. abilities. The first is psychological competence, which is responsible for the relationship of a person with himself.

a) Psychological competences

These abilities include:

Self-esteem - it includes awareness of your pros and cons, as well as making an objective assessment of your capabilities;

Self-awareness, or emotional awareness - is nothing but the awareness of our own emotional states, i.e. what we feel, e.g. "I am angry, happy, scared";

Self-control, i.e. self-regulation - it includes the ability to respond to external stimuli with the help of appropriate emotions, as well as the ability to cope with stress and act in accordance with the values adhered to.

b) *Social competence*

Emotional intelligence also includes social competences, i.e. how we deal with relationships with other people. In this case, we have five abilities, such as:

Empathy or the ability to empathize with the emotional states of others - is a very important and valuable skill, because it allows us to be sensitive towards others, understand what they feel and why they behave in a specific way;

Cooperation - it is the ability to cooperate with others to achieve a common goal, and allows us to work effectively and solve problems;

Leadership - in turn, is the ability to efficiently and effectively lead and manage others: their work and activities but also the ability to build a team, and acquire followers of their views;

Assertiveness - the ability to express one's own views while respecting the views of others; it is an extremely important skill that allows us to be polite but firmly refuse to let others be unpleasant;

Persuasion - this is an important ability that allows you to influence others, namely exerting influence on them, and inclining to certain activities. It is also the ability to alleviate disputes.

c) *Action competences*

The third group of skills is competence to act, i.e. how we perform the tasks entrusted to us. Here, too, three specific skills are distinguished. These are:

Diligence - it is taking responsibility for what we do, performing duties on time and feeling satisfied with the activities performed;

Motivation - it is our commitment to what we do and mobilizing our forces to act for a specific purpose; it also includes initiative and creativity in action;

Adaptability - this is a valuable ability nowadays, including the ability to get used to changes in the environment and to respond positively to these changes: it is treating them as a challenge; it is also the ability to work in stressful conditions.

Features of People with High Emotional Intelligence

How to recognize people with high emotional intelligence? They have certain character traits and actions that allow us to state that these people have very highly developed emotional competences.

- **They talk a lot about emotions.** People with a high level of intelligence have a so-called rich emotional dictionary. This means that they talk a lot about emotions, use their names, and name their emotional states.
- **They are curious about people and the world.** These people show great interest in what is happening around them, willingly meet people, are active, and have a lot of passion.
- **They are born optimists.** A characteristic feature of people with high emotional intelligence is optimism, and it is contagious. These people are joyful and sociable.
- **They are empathic and assertive.** People with high emotional intelligence are lucky

owners of two extremely important features. These areas already mentioned are empathy and assertiveness.

- **They work well in a group**. People with a high degree of emotional intelligence like and work well in a group. This is due to well-developed cooperation skills, empathy, and leadership skills, but without a tendency to dominate.
- **They adapt well to changes**. Emotional intelligence makes us like changes, accept them, and treat them as a kind of challenge. If someone likes change and lacks routine badly, they certainly have a high level of emotional intelligence.
- **They are willing to act.** People with high emotional intelligence are action-oriented. They are activists who enthusiastically respond to all opportunities for improvement and doing something interesting.

Emotional Intelligence in Practice and People

We already know what emotional intelligence is and what its components are, but how does it translate into everyday life? It turns out that this ability is necessary for us in many areas of life and clearly facilitates our daily functioning. People with a high level of emotional intelligence are open, free to contact, assertive, willing to cooperate, tolerant, and polite. They are happy to engage in new activities, adapt easily, and are not afraid of risk. They endure failure and criticism well. They have a realistic view of reality, can soberly look at themselves, seeing their pros and cons. They cope well with stress, react adequately to the situation, and are able to control their emotions. As you can easily guess, the abovementioned skills are desired by employers but also allow us to function satisfactorily in different types of relationships. But what if we don't have all of these abilities and would like to work on our emotional intelligence?

The characteristics and essence of emotional intelligence make it a key factor in the success and development of healthy interpersonal relationships. People with high levels of this trait can recognize and control their emotions and reactions so that they do not influence their judgment, have a positive attitude, as well as understand other people's emotional state. They can, therefore, make good decisions, face difficult situations successfully, and survive adverse conditions.

These people also take risks, have patience and perseverance, confidence in their abilities, and are optimistic. In addition, they have the ability to work effectively within a team, communicate effectively with other people, build long-lasting professional and personal relationships, and are even better suited for positions of power. To a large extent, therefore, a person's future success, both in the professional and personal spheres, as well as his life satisfaction and happiness, lie in the development of his emotional intelligence.

Can Emotional Intelligence Be Learned?

Fortunately, it turns out that emotional intelligence can be improved throughout life. Professional emotional intelligence courses are the most effective today. We can also work independently at home. Let's find a moment for ourselves and our emotions. At this time, let's wonder what emotions we had experienced lately, when and how strong they were. Let's add to this our reactions: "Yesterday I was angry because I had an argument with my fiance. I screamed, and left the house slamming the door." If we can be aware of what we feel, we will be more aware of our emotional states. Then let's go a step further and think about how the people around us feel: "My fiance was also surely angry when we argued, and when I left the house, he would be concerned about what was happening to me." Let's also read the newspapers and let's name emotions on people's faces in photos. Later, it's worth creating scenarios of behavior, for example, wondering how we would behave in a given situation. Our own training of emotions will certainly bring specific results if it is conducted regularly.

How to Measure Emotional Intelligence?

Emotional intelligence is measurable and is measured using a series of standardized psychological tools. The most popular is INTE, i.e., the Emotional Intelligence Questionnaire. These capabilities can also be chopped down with a fairly simple KKS test, i.e., the Social Competence Questionnaire. It examines our behavior in a number of social situations, including close contact with others, a situation that requires assertive behavior, and social exposure, e.g., a public appearance. The tests are used in diagnostics, including in therapeutic work, as well as in broadly understood counseling, e.g., in career counseling.

To sum up: emotional intelligence is needed, it can be measured, and it can be learned. It turns out that it is worth it because people with a high level of emotional intelligence function much better both in private and professional life.

CHAPTER 14
HOW TO DEVELOP EMOTIONAL INTELLIGENCE

1. Developing Emotional Intelligence: Emotional Self-Awareness

Emotional self-awareness means having the ability to recognize, and understand one's emotions and mood. It is an intellectual process, and thanks to it, it is possible to establish a relationship between what you feel, how you express yourself, and how other people receive it. You should focus on yourself to understand yourself a little better.

Thanks to emotional self-awareness, you can identify the concrete emotional states experienced throughout the day so that you can analyze the effect it has around you; these emotions also interfere with social relationships.

For example, on a day when you are happy about making the most of the plans you have with your best friends, it is possible that in a moment of annoyance, you may tend to distance yourself and see the negative side of others. Emotions, in a way, change the way you see the world around you.

2. How to develop emotional intelligence: emotional self-regulation

Also known as emotional self-control, it implies the ability to control impulses and emotions assertively and concretely to avoid living on primary instincts. Low emotional self-regulation can lead to many conflicts, arguments, and fights with those around you. Over time, it can produce a very negative personal image and alienate your close friendships and relationships.

Thanks to emotional self-control, you can regulate emotional responses by reacting appropriately to the events you face in life so that you can better adapt to your surroundings.

It's about learning to think things through before you speak, rationalizing your emotions to keep them from unfolding and turning into anxiety, or getting your own resources to learn how to manage your behavior and emotions with yourself.

3. How to develop emotional intelligence: motivation

Motivation is the third component of emotional intelligence. It is a psychological process that comprises the ability to direct emotional states to a particular objective or goal, always with a positive focus and a lot of energy. Thanks to motivation, it is also possible to easily recover from life's setbacks, find solutions more effectively and refocus on goals, becoming more persistent and emphatic.

For example, if your goal is to get a good job, you may not be able to do it at first, but thanks to your motivation you will never forget what your goal is and will keep looking for the best path until you reach that goal.

The lack of motivation can be translated as boredom, tiredness, the routine understood as negative form, sadness, among others. On the other hand, having a reason to fight becomes fuel for living.

4. How to develop emotional intelligence: empathy

Working with emotional intelligence, the fourth element is empathy. When it comes to empathy, we are talking about the famous ability to put oneself in another's place, to recognize people's emotions and feelings. In more extreme cases, live these emotions.

Thanks to this ability, you are able to understand and internalize the emotions of others from the emotional expression these people show you. Be aware because, with the feelings and emotions of those around you, you can see your surroundings from another perspective. Knowing how another person feels through understanding gestures is a skill that fosters mutual understanding and allows you to have more and better interpersonal relationships.

For example, if someone is crying beside you, you may understand that they are suffering from some kind of pain, whether physical or emotional. But knowing that this happens, and you have developed the ability to be empathic, you can feel this pain as yours.

5. How to develop emotional intelligence: social skills

Finally, working with emotional intelligence has the last point, social skills. Understand social skills as a set of skills that allow you to respond appropriately in different contexts and better relate to the people around you. They are the key to good personal and professional development. Thanks to them, you communicate more assertively, making your needs known so that the people who live with you understand better how you feel.

A good example of social ability is a person who keeps calm and knows how to express opinions and emotions calmly, avoiding conflict. You should not confuse social skills with manipulating people, as in this case there are no lies, blackmail, or psychological abuse.

Working with emotional intelligence

Other factors to keep in mind to work on and strengthen your emotional intelligence are:

Be resilient

Resilience is the ability of human beings to be flexible in the face of difficulties that arise in life. You can build and strengthen your resilience when, for example, at a very complicated time in your life you are able to look ahead and project overcoming in the near future by understanding what steps you should take in different areas of your life. That is, "get out" of yourself, your emotions and work to achieve overcoming.

Be positive

Dealing with life's adversities positively is one of the most important elements of a fulfilling life, knowing how to look at the strengths and learn from any situation makes you stronger and more prepared. This does not mean that you cannot be sad at any time in your life, but knowing how to look at the problem, understanding your feelings, taking action, and being able to learn from it all is critical to a happy life.

Be outgoing

Being able to express feelings is an easier way to develop relationships with people so that they are able to understand what you feel and what your limits are. To achieve this, you should go out with your friends more, meditate, and propose to get out of your comfort zone.

Have self-esteem

Having high self-esteem is a great way for personal development as it enhances mental stability, helps you make tough decisions and prevents numerous anxiety problems. With self-love, you can achieve many of the goals you set for yourself throughout life and especially address those situations that are fearful and susceptible to failure. For this reason, it is so important to work on self-esteem.

Have self-confidence

As we mentioned earlier, it is important to have a well-structured life goal and trust it. However, if you do not have self-confidence and self-esteem, your project may fail because you will be the first to give up. Work on your self-confidence and be constant daily. It is a process that requires patience but is extremely beneficial to your quality of life. But do not confuse self-confidence with pride.

Face the pressure

Today's world is extremely fast and competitive, both in the personal environment such as having the perfect Instagram life as well as in the professional environment because of having to reach goals at the end of the month proposed by the company. However, you should be calm and clearly analyze the situations that present themselves to you.

It is very necessary that you organize and divide your time in a balanced way according to your personal needs, so you will not feel overwhelmed and will perform better in all areas of your life.

Benefits of Emotional Intelligence

Emotional intelligence can be the best predictor of success in life, giving a more accurate definition of being intelligent.

People with above-average emotional quotients (EQs) are generally better able to cope with the demands, pressures, and constraints of everyday life. It gives them a better ability to control their environment by allowing them to:

1. Better adapt, that is, to know how to implement all the solutions, physiological and behavioral to be in adequacy with the whole of our environment—the climatic conditions, society, flora, and resources. Anything that can promote or endanger our existence.

"The species that survive are not the strongest, nor the smartest species, but the ones that best adapt to change." [Charles Darwin]

2. Manage tensions, habitual contributions to the search for performance, and the obligation of result.

Tensions must never become obstacles to our projects, so it is essential to acquire the tools of emotional regulation.

3. Improve understanding of the emotions and feelings of the people we are dealing with and inducing a better quality of listening. This creates a link that will often ease emerging tensions through more effective communication or facilitate conflict resolution.

4. To collaborate better. The ability to collaborate is an important component of emotional intelligence. Like the others, it can be increased. It is possible to develop communication, minimize ego and affect, increase the sense of belonging, and share a common vision.

5. Increase creativity by bringing together in our conscious work area the elements scattered in remote areas of the brain and giving them a new form. For this, it is necessary to solicit the memories inscribed in our senses, and draw on our internal database rich in billions of information. We must also work to determine the most appropriate configuration for the emergence of original concepts by identifying the most productive context, circumstances, postures, the degree of relaxation, receptivity, and concentration.

6. To increase our charisma. "To impose it so as not to have to impose, that is what the charisma is about.

One of the essential components of charisma is seduction.

It is only charisma that seduces. Either by its appearance (the sign of a healthy genetic heritage), but this may not be enough, or by its qualities and abilities.

It is essential to have a sense of self-confidence, to know how to communicate and to have at least one key skill (talent, humor, culture, etc.). It is also important to have high social skills and to be a catalyst for positive emotions.

It can easily be noted that many of these parameters can be developed.

Emotional Intelligence at Work: The 5 Benefits!

1. Improve thinking

Do you believe that reason and emotion are opposite dimensions on the same scale and are always competing to take control of your actions?

This idea makes sense, but it is not entirely right.

If you notice fear or euphoria ahead of a challenge, for example, you may wonder why this feeling arises.

Use emotion like a compass or map to get new information that your logic doesn't recognize.

Other benefits of Emotional Intelligence in this regard are increased focus and concentration.

This avoids distraction with people making malicious comments or sharing irrelevant news, for example.

You will find that these comments and information have no effect on your life, other than stimulating certain negative emotions.

These emotions can be controlled through Emotional Intelligence.

It also helps you solve problems at work without taking them personally, getting faster and less conflicting solutions.

2. Recognize and avoid "emotional kidnappings."

You usually have:

- Tantrums?
- Fight with the people you love?
- Leave important work aside while watching dozens of silly videos?

Moments like this are called emotional kidnappings—when an emotion controls your behavior, and you only realize it after a while.

One of the benefits of Emotional Intelligence is to realize these moments early on.

By noticing these kidnappings quickly, we can then act!

Once you notice them, control the situation quickly and avoid negative behavior, even when there is strong emotion encouraging it.

This is what we might call emotional freedom.

3. Make better decisions in the company.

Emotional kidnapping is the pinnacle of emotional control, but it goes far beyond that, happening in subtle ways in everyday life. Do you:

- Eat a bakery snack before arriving at the company, or before a healthy meal?
- Sleep early, or watch another episode of your favorite series?
- Pay the bills, or buy something you don't need, why did your co-workers buy it too?

All these decisions have an emotional component, even though it is our custom to hide them: desire, curiosity, envy, and so on.

Are you a manager? This further increases the importance of acting intelligently.

Only then can you get the best out of each of your employees!

There is no point in charging a collaborator much when he is greatly stressed.

In this case, you may want to have a quiet conversation with him, try to motivate him or take time for the employee to rest and empty his head.

Emotional Intelligence will help you make better decisions, that is, decisions that meet your long-term goals, not your immediate interests.

4. Build deeper professional relationships.

Recognizing and "managing" your own emotions is a step toward doing this with others and building deeper relationships.

This will enable you to realize what they are feeling, and to respond accordingly—one of the greatest benefits of Emotional Intelligence.

Let's say you arrive at work and find your department mate angry after a problem at work.

This will not always be clear, but the signs will be evident to someone who uses emotional intelligence at work and is able to understand them.

Realizing this emotion, you can help him/her to reduce anger!

Help your colleague have a nice day, for example, instead of getting into a discussion that will deepen the bad feeling, be it his stress or anxiety.

5. Health Benefits.

Developing Emotional Intelligence at work will bring benefits to your physical and emotional health as well.

This is because we will reduce stress and anxiety by not going head-first into negative situations.

This is one of the most important factors, as they not only steal your concentration, making you angry, but can lead to heart and bowel problems, physical exhaustion, and so on.

Therefore, if you fail to apply emotional intelligence to your work environment, your health may suffer, and your performance and professional relationships may be adversely affected.

By making better decisions, you will also take care of your diet as you will have quality sleep and exercise consistently.

In addition, you will avoid risky behaviors:

- distancing that long-awaited job promotion in your area;

- treating someone badly that can hurt you in the company;
- self-medication;
- Carelessness caused by the stress of work.

This will ensure a longer and healthier life!

Roles Of Emotional Intelligence And Teamwork

More and more organizations are realizing that hard skills testing and personality assessments are just not cutting it as tools to use in selecting new hires. As companies begin to realize the importance of social skills like the ability to collaborate and work with a team, they are now looking for those "emotional intelligence" qualities not only in new candidates but in existing staff as well. Emotional intelligence in team building is an absolute must to get the most out of any group of people and here are 7 reasons why.

1. Self Awareness

It is exceptionally difficult to understand the emotions and motivations of others if you don't know yourself first. Persons with a high emotional intelligence can quickly identify their emotions which is the first step in being able to control or manage them. Self-awareness is the basic building block of emotional intelligence.

2. Self control

Being able to recognize your emotion is one thing but being able to control those emotions, particularly in stressful conditions is quite another, The person with a developed EI understands why they feel like they do, which gives them an opportunity to examine the emotion rationally and control it.

3. Innate motivational tendencies

Motivation is a key to team momentum and every member plays a role in providing that motivation. Developed EI manifests itself as positive attitude, persistence and a natural support for others. In short it is infectious and others will follow the lead.

4. Empathy

The person with high emotional intelligence has the ability to understand the emotions in another and empathize with them. They understand people of all walks of life and the impact that different cultures have on decision making processes. Understanding these differences allows the person to accept diversity and not have it serve as a barrier to working together effectively.

5. Highly developed social skills

Essential to team members is a high sense of social skills. Being able to resolve conflicts in a mutually acceptable way is critical to the overall success of the team. Well developed social skills can strongly contribute to collaboration and cooperation which in turn will drive productivity.

6. Social interdependence

When a team is created, it will create an environment of social interdependence and that can be a good or bad thing depending on how it is managed. If the team leader explains that the group will focus on team goals and requires the input of all team members to be successful, the result is a greater effort to collaborate. However if the team is set up as competitors, e.g., "The first one to sell 100 widgets gets a big bonus," then you have a team that consists of individuals with individual goals.

7. EI and team work

Positive and effective relationships between team members have been demonstrated to be the superior emotional setting to drive results. Members who share a bond both professionally and personally will work harder to achieve success for the group than a team where those relationships have not been developed. Developing emotional intelligence through exercises and training can greatly improve the odds of effective team performance.

CHAPTER 15
COMMUNICATION WITHOUT WORDS

Not only what you say, but also what you do not say influences how others perceive you. Communication is largely nonverbal. Even if we are unaware, our body is constantly sending signals to which our counterpart reacts. Here, the face plays a special role, because it is on the face that the emotions of facial expressions are transmitted. Often, one look is enough to see how a fellow human being feels. Even if we become masters of deception in the course of life and in many situations want to hide our true thoughts and feelings, we succeed only to a certain extent. Because so-called micro-expressions give a price for a short moment, which is really going through our heads. Communication involves how you correctly interpret facial expressions in others, use them for yourself, what you recognize, and what your counterpart would like to conceal from you...

A short definition

The term "facial expressions" include different movements of the facial muscles, the eyes, the mouth, the lips, but also the cheeks and the forehead. The decisive factor in facial expressions is that these movements are not due to a specific function, but serve only to express personal emotion.

In principle, therefore, not just every facial irritation is part of facial expressions. For example, anyone who is chewing or speaking is also moving many facial muscles but does so for a clear purpose.

Mimicry, on the other hand, serves non-verbal communication and is, therefore, an essential aspect of interpersonal relationships. Many people feel better when they see someone else's face because it is easier to judge and to assess their intentions. On the phone, this is not possible, so you can easily deceive the other party here.

This is more difficult with direct eye contact. Often one betrays oneself by one's own facial expression or awakens doubt with the other person. But the facial expressions—especially the eyes and the mouth—can do much more, cover the entire spectrum of human emotions and are able to reproduce this impressively accurately.

You should also distinguish the gestures, which are also used to express emotions, but primarily by the use of the entire body, the slopes and arms are executed. In addition, the gestures are easier to control and can be used deliberately to emphasize certain points or arguments or to demonstrate their own refusal, such as arms crossed.

How do we learn to interpret facial expressions?

Each person is able to interpret the facial expressions of another. But why? Hardly anyone has specifically trained in this direction, and this is taught neither in school nor at university (except perhaps in a few degree programs).

Much of the facial expressions, you get to know in early childhood. Various facial expressions are copied from the parents and linked to emotions, so it is known very early on, what a face that is happy or just angry looks like.

In addition, we learn to interpret facial expressions through different experiences in the course of life. The brain stores what kind of facial expressions are shown on the face of a person with whom we have quarreled, who is sad or who looked surprised.

The Seven Basic Emotions

Actually, man is an expert when it comes to recognizing emotions. Just try it yourself. For example, observe your colleagues at lunchtime or look people in the face a little more closely during a walk. Even if you have never seen a person before, you get an impression of the other person's emotional state within a very short time.

This ability was vital to us in earlier times. It warned us of dangers and made togetherness possible. Because people have always lived together in groups, we had to develop an excellent sense of the inner state of others to create a peaceful community and avoid conflicts.

The psychologist, Paul Ekman, discovered in the 1960s that certain emotions are the same all over the world and can be understood by anyone. Ekman studied video footage of indigenous peoples and found that most of his facial expressions are familiar to him and that he can associate them with a specific emotion.

He then traveled to Papua New Guinea to substantiate his assumptions. He lived under the isolated tribe of Fore. Ekman studied their facial expressions and showed them pictures of the facial expressions of people of other origins. The fantastic result: Even the tribe members were able to assign an emotion to the facial expressions, although they had never had anything to do with other people.

With this, Ekman could prove that there are seven basic emotions expressed by a specific facial expression:

1. Surprise

Surprise is the shortest emotional state. When are we surprised? When something unexpected happens, when the course of events suddenly changes. To feel surprised, we must not have the slightest hint of what is going to happen.

The wonder lasts only a few seconds until we understand what happened, then it turns into another emotion, which is the reaction to what surprised us. Then we can also exclaim: "What a nice surprise!" Or "What a nasty surprise!" But the wonder itself has nothing positive or negative.

The joy or sorrow we feel comes only later when we realize what happened, for example, that we received an unexpected visit. Since surprise comes unexpectedly, it is theoretically impossible to hide it.

Surprise is different from when something, for example, a sudden noise, catches us off guard and scares us. In this case, it is a simple physical reflex, which is the exact opposite of surprise. It makes us contract our faces and close ourselves to protect ourselves. When we are surprised instead, we open the face as much as possible; three areas of the face are clearly involved.

The wide-open eyes are often associated with raised eyebrows or wide-open mouths, or both, but they can also appear individually. When we are surprised, we are literally speechless. The chin relaxes and lowers, and the mouth opens wide: how much, depends on the intensity of the emotion.

Surprise can have different degrees of intensity, easily deducible from the mouth. Eyes and eyebrows remain more or less the same, but the more the mouth opens, the more the person is surprised. When you only see the gaping mouth, the feeling is that of being speechless. It can be an automatic expression of real emotion or an intentional sign. When we want to hide what we feel, we often pretend to be surprised.

But since it is a very short expression, in reality, it cannot hide much. A fake surprise can be exposed because it lasts too long. The surprise is the shortest emotion, and it lasts just a few seconds before turning into something else.

2. *Sadness*

Sadness is one of the most enduring emotions. It has more or less intense degrees, up to the pain that one feels for mourning. All emotions have extreme forms (for example, an exaggerated fear is called a phobia). But here we talk about everyday expressions.

Many factors can make us sad; one of the most common is to lose something. It may be a matter of losing your job, losing a friend or partner, mourning, etc. Sadness also has a social function: those who show that they are sad can get help, consolation, and support from others.

For some reason, we all grew up with the idea that we shouldn't show that we are sad; when we experience this emotion, many do everything to conceal it. But it does not mean that they always succeed because as much as we try to repress an emotion, our face betrays us.

In the most extreme forms, the only sign of sadness can be the total absence of muscular tone in the face. But often the eyes and forehead are also involved. The inner corners of the eyebrows approach and lift. It is one of the most complex muscle movements to perform voluntarily.

The movement of the eyebrows causes vertical wrinkles to appear or stand out above the nose; also, the inner corner of the upper eyelids rises and takes a triangular shape.

A sad mouth is often interpreted as an expression of contempt. The corners of the mouth stretch downwards and/or the lower lip protrudes into a grimace. When we feel contempt, we raise our upper lip instead; the corner of the mouth points downwards, but the lower lip is not extended.

If someone is pretending to be sad, he will use his mouth and look down. The absence of expressions of sadness in the eyes, in the eyebrows and on the forehead is a great clue to discover the bluff. To be sure that the expression is authentic, one must observe the upper eyelid in a triangle. If someone tries to conceal sadness, he will try hard to control his mouth.

3. *Anger*

We feel anger when someone or something prevents us from getting what we want by putting sticks in the wheels. And we get even angrier if the obstacle is designed specifically for us. But we can also be frustrated when things do not work as they should, which is another way of being sabotaged. Sometimes we get angry with ourselves too. Another cause may be violence or threat: then we feel anger and fear together. Obviously, we get angry with those who treat us poorly and betray us.

Pure anger does not last long, and often joins other emotions, like fear and contempt. Anger is the most dangerous emotion because it can lead us to wish to harm, physically or psychologically, the person who made us lose our temper. It is an impulse that manifests itself at an early age and that we must learn to dominate over the years.

It is often best to avoid acting when you are angry because the emotion interferes with our perceptions. In reality, in these cases, it is better to remain still, to shut up and do nothing until the emotion begins to fade, and we start to perceive everything in a more detailed way.

If we suffer some threat, anger causes fear, which can paralyze us. Anger, on the other hand, leads us to face danger. When we are angry, the eyebrows approach and lower. This movement in itself can mean several things: the person is angry but tries to hide it; he is slightly irritated and is about to get angry; he is serious and is concentrating; he is confused.

If someone makes this gesture while we talk to them, without any problem occurring, it is a sign that we must explain ourselves more clearly. Darwin called it "the muscle of difficulties," which we use when we are confronted with something complex or incomprehensible.

When you are angry, your eyelids tend, and your eyes take on a penetrating look. The lower eyelids may be more or less raised depending on the intensity of the emotion. If someone takes this look without other signs, it means that he is controlling his anger, or that he is trying to concentrate.

To be sure that the expression indicates anger, we must also observe the mouth. There are only two types of angry mouths. The one closed with tight lips, which is used during physical confrontations and fighting or when one tries to refrain from saying something, and the open one, which appears when one speaks of one's anger (and when one screams).

The tightened mouth is, however, one of the first signs that appear when one begins to feel anger. It is easy to see the tension along the jaw: it often manifests itself, even before we realize we are angry. If someone tries to hide his anger, the tension in his eyelids, his gaze, and his eyebrows will betray him.

4. Fear

Fear is caused by a danger that threatens us physically or psychologically. It is unleashed automatically when some object comes to us quickly, or when we lose our balance and risk falling. Many are afraid of snakes and reptiles or going to the dentist. Fear can affect both the physical and psychological levels.

Biologically, fear makes us ready to hide or escape. Blood flows to the main leg muscles, ready to run if necessary. If we don't run, we try to hide, behaving exactly like rabbits caught in car headlights: we remain immobile.

This is because predators with weak eyes do not see prey if it does not move, so the rabbit hides when it remains motionless. When we say "being paralyzed by fear," we are actually hiding.

If we do not run away or hide, the fear is likely to turn into anger that drives us to action to face the threatening situation.

When we are afraid, the eyebrows rise but remain horizontal. The eyes are wide open; the upper eyelids are raised while the lower eyelids are contracted. The mouth is open or ajar, and the lips are tense or thin. If someone pretends to be afraid, he will forget to use his eyebrows and forehead, and probably also his eyes and will simply use his mouth.

The only case in which the forehead and eyebrows are not involved in an expression of genuine fear is when it is a paralyzing emotion, as in the case of a shock. Only the eyes and mouth are involved.

5. *Disgust*

A distancing characterizes disgust. The most common cause of disgust is bodily secretions: excrement, blood, vomit, and other fluids. The reaction occurs only when they are outside the body. You also feel disgusted with certain odors or when we touch something slimy. Some actions are disgusting like animal violence or pedophilia.

Adults think they are disgusted by the behavior of others: immoral people, politicians, tyrants, etc. But what is morally wrong varies from culture to culture.

The disgust is expressed by the curled nose and the raised upper lip. The lower lip can be raised and extended, tightening the mouth, or lowered and extended, opening it. If the disorder is very strong, the eyebrows can be reduced, but they are not very important in this emotion.

Being an obvious expression, it is easy to pretend disgust, and we often do it to accompany a speech. Since the forehead and eyebrows are not significant for this expression, we do not notice their absence in the case of fake emotion. For this reason, it is an emotion that is easy to mask as it mainly uses the lower part of the face. Usually, we don't even bother to hide this emotion.

6. *Contempt*

Disdain has much in common with disgust, but there are some essential differences. We feel contempt for others and their actions, but not for things.

There is also a sort of socio-cultural contempt from the bottom up, such as what young people feel towards adults or the poorly educated towards academics.

Those who are insecure about their position and status often use contempt as a weapon. Many take advantage of their power to show contempt for those who are subordinate to them. It is a very effective method even if then we find ourselves alone at the top hated by all.

Our face expresses contempt by locking and lifting only one corner of the mouth, like a kind of half-smile and or raising only half of the upper lip, like a half expression of disgust.

It can occur discreetly with a slight trembling of the upper lip, or more intensely, by uncovering the teeth. The eye tends to point down; we look down on the person we despise.

If this expression is a natural part of your face, because you were born that way, you will be easily labeled as arrogant and opinionated.

7. Joy

Positive emotions are numerous but currently, we do not have sufficient terms to describe them. For now, we must be content with words like joy or happiness.

An authentic smile involves two essential muscles: the zygomatic major, which raises the corners of the mouth, and the eyes orbicular that relaxes the area around the eyelids. In this way, the eyes are tightened a little, the skin under the lower eyelids is stretched, the eyebrows are lowered, and folds appear on the sides of the eyes.

We can intentionally control the zygomatic major, but this does not apply to the muscles around the eyes. When this muscle is active, we say that someone "smiles with their eyes." The fact that we are unable to control the eyes orbicular makes it easy to recognize a fake smile. In an authentic smile, the eyebrows are slightly lowered, something that nobody can reproduce voluntarily.

If we don't want to be discovered when we pretend to be happy, we have to make the widest possible smile. Then the changes caused by the eye muscles also take place: a wide smile pushes up the cheeks making the skin curl under the eyes; in this way, the eyelids tighten, and wrinkles appear on the sides. It then becomes more challenging to understand whether the smile is sincere or not: the only indication is the eyebrows and the skin below, as the eye muscles lower with a genuine smile.

Ekman developed a system for deciphering and describing facial expressions. It's called the "Facial Action Coding System," FACS for short, and it describes a total of 44 small facial muscle movements. This system helps to detect emotions and makes it possible to interpret facial expressions.

Micro-Expressions Show the True Feelings

How do Paul Ekman's findings help in everyday life? In our daily routine, we are programmed to hide our feelings. You are to smile, although you are not feeling well. You are to agree, although you feel rejected. But the facial muscles are directly linked to the limbic system, the emotional center. Thus, it is not possible to completely hide our feelings.

In a facial expression shorter than the duration of a blink of an eye, feelings flash for a moment. These are the so-called micro-expressions.

They come to light because the limbic system processes information faster than the cerebrum, thereby tearing us away from controlling one's own emotions for a moment. Uncontrollable reflects on the face reveal for a moment the truth that we really feel. Only then can the mask be put on again.

Especially in situations that touch one emotionally, for example, when it comes to a topic that is important to you, micro expression intensifies. A contradiction in what someone says and what someone thinks and feels is only apparent in this brief moment.

Mimic Point: Error Reading Faces

We should not underestimate how difficult it can be to read a facial expression correctly. A small muscle movement can have different meanings, and the differences are often minimal, increasing the likelihood of a mistake and illustrating how much exercise may be necessary to interpret the facial expressions of others unerringly.

A complete picture is a combination of facial expressions, gestures, and posture. To properly interpret the countenance of the other person, be sure to avoid these mistakes:

1. Isolation

You may have heard that it can be a telltale sign of a lie when someone grabs your narrative. But it could just itch on the nose. Meaning: a single gesture reveals nothing. Only when similar signals accumulate in the facial expressions, it becomes a sign.

So consider a single facial expression never isolated. This merely increases the risk of interpreting something in the other person's facial expression, which is not there at all.

2. Context

Do not just try to interpret the nonverbal language, but always see it in context: What background does your counterpart have? Is the person under particular pressure? Doesn't he like the room? Or what experiences does the person have with such situations already collected?

Depending on the context, facial expressions can mean something different and should be judged accordingly differentiated. Here, it helps to know the other person better to assess the differences in the face between normal behavior and the current situation.

3. Blindness

Do you know the halo effect that was discovered in the 19th century by the American behavioral scientist, Edward Lee Thorndike? It describes a perceptual error in which individual characteristics of a person are so dominant on us that they produce an over shining overall impression.

For example, students with glasses look smarter to many teachers. And that's exactly the problem: you always interpret facial expressions through your own glasses—and that can be cloudy if your perception plays a trick on you that do not notice.

Facial Expressions: How Do I Know That My Counterpart Is Keeping Something From Me?

Recognizing this contradiction can help one understand one's counterpart. At work, this ability is a crucial advantage. For example, talking to a customer about a new suggestion will help you find out if they are positive or negative about it.

Certain signals in the face point you in discussions to objections, doubts, or rejection. However, it should be told in advance that the recognition of these signals requires intensive training. You will not immediately recognize them, if only because they only show up in the face of your counterpart for a fraction of a second.

These signals express doubts and objections:

Raising the eyebrows

If the eyebrows of a conversation partner shoots skyward, this unconsciously expresses skepticism. It shows that he is not yet convinced of what you say. It can also be a sign of new life. If the eyebrows are raised only slightly, your counterpart will signal interest.

The lips apron

This may mean that your correspondent thinks about your proposal and weighs it up. But it can also mean that your opponent is considering another proposal.

The eyebrows contract

This signal is an expression that your counterpart is concentrated. However, if I pull the eyelids up, annoyance is signaled.

These signals express rejection:

Pulling up the upper lip

An upper lip shows that your opponent assesses the situation differently than you. Being aware of this while suggesting or explaining something may mean that your interviewee disagrees with you.

The nose up

Those who sniff the nose up signal that something does not suit them. This signal can also mean that your counterpart thinks what you propose is difficult to implement.

If you can observe one of these signals with your correspondent, let this observation flow into the conversation. For example, you could say, "I see you still have doubts." You can then talk to the interlocutor and have the chance to convince him. In addition, you prove your empathy.

Facial Expressions: How They Influence Us

As a non-verbal communication, facial expressions have a very direct influence on how other people perceive and judge us. How much this works, everyone can experience for themselves. Imagine, for example, meeting a new colleague or meeting new people at a party, where rejection is virtually written on their faces. With all the effort, you will hardly succeed to perceive them as sympathetic or even make friends.

It is very different when someone is open, friendly, positive, and has inviting facial expressions. It makes you feel welcome, builds a good rapport, and you keep talking. Even a smile and eye contact can be enough to attract fellow human beings and break the ice.

But facial expressions influence not only the behavior and emotions of other people. You can also use your facial expressions in a targeted manner to improve your own mood or even become more self-confident. How does it work? Simple: smile—even if you have no reason to.

Whether you feel like a smile beaming with joy or not, it makes no difference to the brain. It moves the same facial muscles and sends the same signals to the brain, which produces happiness hormones. In this way, you can put yourself in a better and more optimistic mood, from which you can achieve better results and performance.

However, this also works the other way around, which is why you need to pay attention to your negative facial expressions. Running around with doubts on your face all the time makes them more and more solid in their own attitudes and impacting on all aspects of life.

If you want to use your facial expressions deliberately to improve your mood, we recommend the cozy atmosphere at home. You may feel funny at first with the artificial smile, but the effect is worthwhile. In addition, such an applied smile in the facial expressions may be negative to other people. If you do not really feel like you're having fun, it's best to just smile for yourself—after that, the world usually looks very different.

CHAPTER 16

EMPATHY A GREAT GIFT AND CURSE. WHAT TO DO WITH EMPATHY?

Currently, much importance is given to learning to take care of our mind in order to enjoy a good state of health, both physical and mental.

Two aspects in Western culture, until relatively recently, did not seem so close and in recent years have been approaching, making it almost impossible to imagine a good state of physical health without the company of good mental health and vice versa.

The recommendations to achieve and maintain this emotional well-being are endless, even so, sometimes we forget the simplest and the ones we have the most within reach. But that doesn't mean we should stop cultivating. Empathy is the ability that people have to perceive, tune in, connect and understand the emotions and feelings of others, as described by Anna Forés and Eva Bach. This ability is not innate and is acquired throughout life, which opens the door to thinking that it will be necessary to pay special attention if we want it to develop properly.

In the early 1990s, it was discovered that this ability came from neurons known as "mirror neurons." These, capturing the nonverbal emotional signals of the other people with whom we interact, allow us to reproduce their feelings and actions by observing them, just as babies imitate their parents' gestures.

Positive social relationships help us to achieve the desired state of well-being and this does not only come from the fact that we feel good about ourselves by establishing good links with those around us, but also, by doing so, we release hormones and neurotransmitters such as Oxytocin, which facilitate us to reach this state and maintain good physical and mental health.

Francesc Torralba described that it is not the amount of relationships that gives meaning to our lives, but the quality of the links, the delicacy of the treatment we are able to dispense. To achieve these relationships and quality links that will lead us towards emotional well-being, we have a great help: empathy. It is necessary to know that this help will have to be worked for to achieve its correct functioning and to extract its maximum potential.

Etymologically, there is a similarity between empathy and sympathy, although these two are not in any case the same. Sympathy means feeling the same as the other and if not, there is a feeling of pity or sorrow about the other person. Empathy, on the other hand, tries to get closer to what the other is feeling without letting their emotions be confused with their own, pretending to understand the feelings of the other person even while being aware that they are different from those of oneself.

We must understand that to be empathic, it is not necessary to find solutions to all the problems that those who approach us present. Sometimes it is enough to listen silently and respectfully to the person who opens up to us and let him know that we are available for him. You need to avoid giving advice if he does not request them. In this way, the person feels supported, while understanding that our feelings and emotions are different.

If we are aware of these concepts and take care of them just as we take care of our body when we exercise, our social behaviors will improve and consequently our relationships, making them deeper and more sincere and thus giving us a chemical rain of emotional well-being.

Unconscious Empathy vs. Conscious Empathy

Empathy is the ability to put on the skin of other people.

There are people who have a much more developed empathy because of their personal characteristics.

In principle, being empathetic is positive because it allows you to better understand others and therefore feel closer to them.

There are professions in which being empathetic is an indispensable quality. Caregivers, therapists, psychologists, doctors, social workers and all the workers who accompany and help others, usually possess this ability, which on the other hand greatly facilitates their work.

So far so good.

But it is also important to know that empathy can at any given time harm us instead of helping us.

An excess of empathy can play against instead of in favor…

Not long ago I took a course that I loved, it was about how to acquire self-care skills and it was intended for people who work in the field of helping other people.

The content of what I learned was broad, practical and experiential. I could count many things, but in this chapter, I will focus on one of the aspects that were discussed at the beginning of the same and that I think is important to share: differentiating between conscious and unconscious empathy.

Unconscious empathy

Unconscious empathy makes us feel confused with each other due to an excess of involvement.

From that confusion, we do not know how to modulate or manage what we feel, that is, we do not know how to regulate the emotions that the other awakes in us. It is then when the emotional contagion occurs or said more grossly: I permeate the emotions of the other person.

If you do not know how to drive these emothions, they can take a toll on you, because the emotions of the other will become yours. You will not know how to differentiate between yours and the other person's emotions.

From this place, it is difficult to observe to regulate or manage emotions.

If you do not learn to empathize consciously, it is easy to end up dragging a backpack of emotions that do not belong to you but that you unconsciously make yours.

That is why it is important to learn to empathize consciously...

Conscious empathy

Empathizing consciously consists of being present for the other person, but from a prudent distance. This is achieved by adopting the role of an objective and attentive observer.

In this way you will be much more aware of what the other person awakens in you and you can regulate the emotions that can emerge effectively. There are different ways to regulate yourself emotionally, but they are not the objective of this chapter, I will talk about it later.

The aim of conscious empathy is to be empathic but without getting too involved so as not to lose perspective, an essential requirement to help the other person.

Conscious empathy is finding the degree of involvement necessary to accompany the other without feeling dragged or overwhelmed by their emotions.

In summary: with unconscious empathy you run the risk of emotional contagion, but with conscious empathy you can learn to keep a distance, manage yourself and release emotions that do not belong to you.

CHAPTER 17
STRATEGIES TO LIVE BETTER

A person with high empathy suffers continuous emotional contagion. One way to establish a healthier limit is to strengthen our empathy, that is, to be able to connect, but excluding from us the impregnation of the feelings of others.

Walt Whitman said in a poem that he didn't usually ask the injured person how he felt, because when he looked at it, he himself became a suffering soul. We do not know if the famous author of *Leaves in the Grass* was highly empathic, but in these two lines he summed up perfectly a reality that many people live.

There are those who see this subject as something strange, even contradictory. How can empathy, that ability to put ourselves in other people's shoes, sometimes become something painful? Basically, because there are those who, as if it were an antenna, capture each and every one of the emotions of others. But this is not all; they are impregnated with sorrows and pains that are not their own, realities that are not theirs live on their skin... and they suffer in the same way.

Thus, while the act of feeling sorry and compassionate is something to be expected in the human being, there are those who push that connection to the limit until it becomes something traumatic. In the most extreme cases, we would even be talking about a clinical condition known as the syndrome of excessive empathy or compassionate wear. The diagnostic and statistical manual of mental disorders (DSM-V) labels it as a category of personality disorders.

It is not easy to live in a world where one cannot put a healthy barrier between the "self" and the "I" of others. So let's see what strategies we can carry out to live better.

"The ability to place oneself in the place of the other is one of the most important functions of intelligence. It shows the degree of maturity of the human being."

-TO. Cury

Be highly empathic, when the connection leads to suffering

Knowing how to respond to the anguish of others with well-regulated empathy is a key to well-being. However, no one has taught us to control or handle it; we grope and react to the emotional realities of others with greater or lesser success. Now, something that several studies show us is that we must learn to use it effectively. The goal is to make empathy an interpersonal skill.

Thus, studies such as those carried out at the University of Cambridge by Dr. Erin B. Tone, for example, point us to something interesting. There is a genetic propensity towards empathic sensitivity. That is, being highly empathic is something we can be born with. In addition, it has been shown that excess empathy, both emotional and cognitive, can lead to internalizing disorders.

Therefore, realities such as the feeling of anguish, fear, guilt or unhappiness can be due precisely to emotional "contagions." On the other hand, works such as those carried out at the institute of psychiatry at King's College in London, inform us of very similar data.

While low empathy is linked to people with clear difficulties in social interaction or with an autism spectrum disorder, those who suffer from excess empathy suffer from emotional exhaustion. This state, and the clear difficulty in processing other people's emotions, affects, in many cases, the mental health of the person.

How can we handle these realities a little better? We analyze it below.

Listen to words, avoid creating images in your mind

Being highly empathic has, on average, a curious faculty. To understand it better, we will give an example: a friend of yours tells you that he is suffering from mobbing at work.

Your mind visualizes each scene, coworkers humiliating and stalking him, and your friend suffering in solitude, persistent anxiety... Each word heard becomes an image and, in this way, you connect even more with the suffering and take it with you.

As far as possible, you should focus only on words, preventing them from appearing in your mind in the form of an image.

Empathy, protection mechanism against emotional contagion

Empathy wins, more than when it is known, when it is applied. This term was proposed by the doctor and professor of psychiatry, JL González. It is a cognitive and an emotional strategy by which we avoid that the emotions of others drag us. To do this, we must internalize the following:

- Empathy does not fit into other people's shoes to understand how others feel. It is to stay where we are and make an empathic round trip: I observe, connect and return unscathed to my position.
- It is a mental ability to manage any contagion and thus be able to provide useful and effective support. Because remember, if I am infected by the same anguish of those who suffer, I will not be of any use.
- Dr. JL González de Rivera indicates that empathy forces us at any given time to turn around the concept of empathy. That is, when we discover the emotional reality of others, we must choose to exclude from ourselves the feelings, attitudes, emotions and motivations that this person experiences. I remain with mine, evenly.

Visualize how you let each other's emotions go inside
Being highly empathic implies, as we know, to stay with the reality of who we have in front of us. If they suffer, I suffer, if they are worried and anxious, I also experience that state. As we can well

imagine, it is not easy to live like this; Emotional exhaustion is extreme.

Thus, one last simple and elementary strategy is to make use of visualization. Once we connect with what the other experiences, we will visualize a dandelion. Simply blow a little and let everything that has adhered to us come off. Little by little, the pain, anguish, and stress ease up... Everything is left out and we are free, strong and prepared to support the other, to give him the best of us.

To conclude, if we identify with this type of profile, we do not hesitate to apply these simple tips. Let's make empathy an effective and healthy resource.